Life in the Eyes of Thatha

by

Dr. Radha Krishna Rao Yarlagadda
Emeritus professor
School of Electrical and Computer Engineering
Oklahoma State University, Stillwater, Oklahoma 74078

DORRANCE
PUBLISHING CO
EST. 1920
PITTSBURGH, PENNSYLVANIA 15238

Dorrance Publishing Co
585 Alpha Drive
Pittsburgh, PA 15238
Visit our website at *www.dorrancebookstore.com*

ISBN: 978-1-4809-4945-4
eISBN: 978-1-4809-4922-5

To My Grandchildren, Present and Future

Dear Ones,

I want you to be happy and proud of your heritage. In my seventy-nine years of living, I went through difficult times with health and adversities. I am grateful to my family, relatives, and friends who have been kind to me and overlooked my many mistakes and faults. I learned some lessons about life empirically that are included in the main part of the book. A few personal suggestions are given below that might be helpful to you.

1. Be kind to yourself, to your family, to your friends, and to the ones who depend on you. Be proud that you were born in this great country and a citizen of USA. Nurture your relationships. When your parents become old, be kind to them. Be flexible, learn to compromise, and give proper deference to seniors. Follow the Bible saying (Proverbs 15:1): *"A soft answer turns away wrath, but a harsh word stirs up anger."* Be polite to the ones that are less fortunate than you are.

2. Have an appreciation for one of the American Indian Prayers: *"Great Spirit, grant that I may not criticize my neighbor until I have walked a mile in his moccasins."* Treat people with dignity and respect. Follow through your promises to yourself, your family, and friends. Think before you speak! You are accountable for your actions. Do not personalize differences with anyone. The heaviest thing to carry is a grudge. It is toxic. Dispose of it. Forgiveness is a gift you give it to yourself.

3. Everyone makes mistakes and goes through disappointments. That is a part of life. Do not make a new mistake to undo an earlier one. Learn from your mistakes.

4. Have patience, keep your mind active, and use your mind wisely. William Penn[1] states, *"Patience and Diligence, like Faith, move Mountains."* Keep good working relationships with your colleagues, and staff. Find a profession that interests you. Have a good work ethic and pride in your work; do your best; be consistent; make use of all your resources; and deliver what you promised. Work towards long-term benefits, not short-term benefits. Follow the saying of Mahatma Gandhi, *"Live as if you were to die tomorrow; learn as if you were to live forever."*

5. Do not compare yourself with others. Follow your own standards. Focus on items that make a difference. Good education and persistence are necessary for any one's success. Knowledge is not inherited. It has to be learned and improved. Cultivate your creativity by asking questions. Nobel Laureate Dr. Albert Einstein[2] said, *"Imagination is more important than knowledge. Knowledge is limited. Imagination encircles the world."* In dealing with anyone, trust, but verify. Expect the unexpected. Smiles are beneficial; frowns are detriment to your health.

6. Time is precious. Don't procrastinate. No one can provide you with a blue print for your life. Develop your own plans. There are no guarantees or reset buttons in life. Be a person of integrity. No one can buy respect. It can only be earned. Luck favors the prepared. Learn to live within your means. Creditors dictate. Get into business only if you have business acumen. No one likes to be controlled by anyone or any substance. Be your own man and be in control of yourself. Do not use alcohol, tobacco, or illicit drugs, as they can ruin your life.

7. Lastly, I appreciate you calling me *Thatha* (Grandfather in Telugu, the language of my native tongue). I look forward to seeing you. This book is dedicated to you.

Thatha

Preface

My family has been my life. I do not consider myself successful in every aspect of my life, nor do I know the best paths in life. I keep going, one-step at a time. I try to improve myself and do the best to help others. I do not blame others for my failures.

People in this country are competitive and generous. They recognize, respect, and attract individuals with good intellect, talent, and work ethic regardless of their ethnicity or national origin to be part of the work force. If one is willing to work hard, he/she can write his/her own script in achieving his/her goals. Following describes life in general.

The Masterpiece
'The more the marble wastes,
The more the statue grows.'
Life has chipped me and chiseled me. Great hunks of self-assurance, pride, willfulness, have been knocked off. The hammer has been cruel and the chisel has cut deep. Wastes of my arrogance, my ambition, my conceit, lie at my feet. A desolate sight if it were not that I keep in mind the two little lines that began this article.
'The more the marble wastes,
The more the statue grows.'
In shaping a beautiful character, in making a masterpiece out of you, life must waste you. Without it you would remain a crude chunk of humanity. Your trials are the hammer, your tribulations the chisel. Together they make you or break you.

Life is chiseling away, hacking at you. It depends on your courage whether the finished product will be divine, a work of art, or just another one of life's atrocities.

Mildred Seydell[3]

My Brief History

I was born in 1938 in Velpucherla, Andhra Pradesh (AP), a southern state in India, to a loving middle-class Hindu Yarlagadda family. Hinduism is the oldest "*known*" recorded religion. My family, in India called me by "*Krishna*" and here by "*Rao*." My parents—father, Yarlagadda China Ghantiah and mother, Yarlagadda (*née* Manam) Sobhanachalamma—are deceased in 1968 and 1979, respectively (We were thankful my mother visited us in Stillwater, OK, to see two of her grandchildren.). My father's father died when my father was only three months old. My ancestors were land owners and some were village munsifs (tax collectors). The crops on my father's lands were rice, tobacco, and others. Since there were no schools beyond elementary school in my village in the 1940s, my parents decided that I live with my sister Gutta Narayanamma and her family during school years, as I would have good educational opportunities. What a wonderful personal sacrifice my parents made for my future, considering my brothers, Chandram and Venkataratnam, died before I was born. My sister took tender care of me for over ten years. My brother-in-law, Dr. Gutta Kutumba Rao, a physician and a disciple of Mahatma Gandhi, helped me in getting my higher education. I am grateful. My sister and brother-in-law are now deceased. During three years of my middle school, I stayed with my aunt Korlipara Varalakshmamma and uncle, Korlipara Kasi Vishwanath Venkatachalam's family. My wife, Marceil Elaine Henney was born in 1942 to DeLoy W. (of Irish and German descent) and Helen (*née* Sykora, of Czech descent) Henney, a Michigan Christian farm family. She received her B.S. from the Central Michigan University (1965) and taught high school mathematics for a year in Michigan. We were married in 1966 and have three children: Tammy Jill, Ryan Ghantiah DeLoy, and Travis Troy. As of 2016, we have five grandchildren that my wife and I adore.

Education, Teaching and Managing Life: I received my B.E. in electrical engineering from the University of Mysore in India (1959). I came to USA in 1960 after working for a year in India as a Junior Electrical Engineer, AP Electricity Board. Before I came to this country, I was worried about getting admitted to one of the universities in this country. Noting my concern, my father said, "*Do not fret. You can manage our lands and live comfortably at home.*" I learned from my father that diversifying in several activities gives more choices in life. I used that idea in every aspect of my life. Even though my parents were not educated beyond elementary school, they had a strong faith in education. My mother was influential in my desire to learn and help others.

I received my M.S. from the South Dakota State University in 1961 and PhD from the Michigan State University in 1964, both in electrical engineering. As a Research Assistant under Dr. Yilmaz Tokad, my PhD thesis advisor, I learned the basics of research. I taught at Tennessee Technological University during 1964-1966; then, I joined Oklahoma State University (OSU) and retired from OSU in 2006. Teaching permitted me to work with students to help themselves to be successful in life. It was a pleasure. I believed in the Chinese saying, "*One learns most from teaching others.*" I was pleased when 21 of the 30 PhD students I worked with came to Stillwater, OK, from all over the country to celebrate my retirement, a total surprise to me. They established the R. K. Rao Yarlagadda Graduate Scholarship Fund to support graduate students in the signal processing area. My research interests were in analysis of signals that includes speech, seismic, and image signals, and design of communication systems. I received one of the Burlington Northern Faculty Achievement Awards at OSU in 1987. I was elected in 1999 as a Fellow of the Institute of Electrical and Electronics Engineers (IEEE) *for research and contributions to education in digital signal processing.*

Summer Employments: I spent fourteen summers at various companies and research laboratories in this country. These were Loewer, Sargent & Associates (Kensington, MD, 1965), Bell Laboratories (Holmdel, NJ, 1967; North Andover, MA, 1971; Whippany, NJ, 1976; and Murray Hill, NJ, 1978), Collins Radio Co., (Dallas, TX, 1969), AMOCO Research (Tulsa, OK, 1979), Institute for Telecommunication Sciences, U.S. Department of Commerce (Boulder, CO, 1980, 1981, 1982, and 1983), Naval Ocean Systems Center (San Diego, CA, 1988), and General Electric Corporate Research and Development (Schenectady, NY, 1990 and 1997). Summer employments helped me to broaden my technical background and collaborate with engineers and scientists. It is refreshing. I found out what it means to be in someone else's lab as a short-timer. In addition, summers allowed for quality time with my family and see this great country.

Research Funds: I was funded as a Principal Investigator by several U.S. governmental agencies. These include, National Science Foundation (A New Approach to Network Synthesis; Hypercube-Instrumentation), the U.S. Army Research Office (Image Coding and Speaker Recognition), Sandia National Laboratories (Special Signal Processing for Day/Night Linear Array Imager; Coding, Data Synchronization, and Encryption), U.S. DOD/National Security Agency (Speech Coding and Speaker Authentication), U.S. Air Force (An Adaptive Approach to a 2.4 kb/s LPC Speech Coding System), and the Office of Naval Research (Parallel Implementation of L_p Algorithms). I was the Project Director of the Consortium of Oil and Well Service Companies on Data Enhancement of Well Logs via Signal Processing at OSU for about ten years. The funding members were AMOCO, ARCO, BP, Cities Service, CONOCO, Dresser-Atlas, EXXON, Gearhart, IBM, Mobil, OXY USA, Phillips, Schlumberger, Seismograph Service Corporation, SOHIO, and Texaco with varied time intervals of support by companies. It was a joint project between the Schools of Electrical and Computer Engineering and Geology, and the Department of Physics at OSU. Other research funds came from ERICO Inc., (Digitization of Logs), and Texas Instruments (AWS Image Processing Techniques). Funds were used for research and support graduate students. I am grateful for the support.

Major Illnesses and Recovery: During my childhood, I had rheumatic fever reducing the effectiveness of my heart. Dr. Denton Cooley, a renowned heart surgeon from the Texas Heart Institute, replaced my aortic and mitral heart valves by mechanical valves. I had a stroke during surgery. My wife was informed that my chances of survival were minimal. After the surgery, some of my attending physicians gave me tests that included adding integers. I had trouble. I worried about my family with children at home. I built my physical strength by walking and strengthened my memory by thinking about the past, present, and the future. I recovered physically and mentally. My brain took its own time in the recovery process. Our memory makes us who we are! George Santayana said, *"We must welcome the future, remembering that soon it will be the past; and we must respect the past, remembering that it was once all that was humanly possible."*

Writing Books: I coauthored three books: *Data Transportation and Protection*, Plenum Press, 1986 (490 pages); *The Elements of System Design*, Academic Press, 1994 (280 pages); *Hadamard Matrix Analysis and Synthesis with Applications to Communications and Signal/Image Processing*, Kluwer Academic Publishers, 1997 (123 pages). Doing research, writing books, and serving as one of the Founding Editors of Signal processing, A Review Journal (Academic Press, 1991-1997) with my friend, Dr. John Hershey was a pleasure and a learning experience. After my heart valve surgery recovery, I started working on the book *Analog and Digital Signals and Systems* (540 pages), a text book published in 2010 by Springer. It is translated into Chinese by Prof. Zhoumo Zeng et al from Tianjin University, China. It is published by China Machine Press in 2017. Prof. Zeng and his associates spent a phenomenal amount of time and a herculean effort in doing the translation. I am grateful to them. I am honored and humbled by the translation.

This project would not have materialized without the help of Prof. Weili Zhang at OSU. Weili, being an educator and a scholar, felt that the Chinese translation of my book would be useful to the students in China. He contacted Prof. Zeng about my book and encouraged him to translate the book. My heartfelt thanks to Weili.

I typed a third of the manuscript of my most recent book on my PC in the mid-1990s. When my PC slowed down due to the manuscript and research data, I asked a technician to help. He reformatted the hard drive. Unfortunately, I did not have a backup of the hard drive. Back in those days, backing up a hard drive would take a stack of floppies and patience to do backup. I lost the latest version of the typed manuscript along with computer programs. I searched my soul how to continue redoing my book manuscript. My mottos were and still are: *"Never give up; never feel sorry for myself; take one step at a time in achieving my goals; plan for the worst scenario in any endeavor; hope for the best; and be helpful to others."* I followed the Serenity Prayer. A portion of it follows.

The Serenity Prayer
"God grant me the serenity to accept the things I cannot change;
courage to change the things I can;
and wisdom to know the difference…

Reinhold Niebuhr[4]

Why I Wrote this Manuscript? I took solace in writing my thoughts and reflections, meditations on life, from what I learned as a family man, a neighbor, a professor and an adviser to many students, a researcher, and one who had gone through severe illnesses and adversities. Following is a nice quote etched on the wall at the Texas Heart Institute.

Isn't it Strange?

Isn't it strange, that princes and kings,
and clowns that caper in sawdust rings,
and common-folk like you and me,
are builders for eternity?
To each is given a bag of tools,
a shapeless mass and a book of rules;
and each must make 'ere time has flown,
a stumbling block or a stepping stone.
R. L. Sharpe, *"A bag of tools,"* circa 1809

Acknowledgments

Thanks to Mrs. Sandra Cohlmia who edited one of the earlier versions of this manuscript. I am grateful for all the help I received from my relatives during early part of my life. My Guardian Angel(s) looked after me during illnesses, and when I had a bike accident with a bus in India and a car accident with a tractor-trailer in Tennessee.

My wife started on her master's program at OSU in mathematics in 1966. After finishing half the courses towards her master's degree, she sacrificed her teaching career to be a stay-home mom to raise our children and give me support. My children gave me the love and respect. My daughter, Tammy Yarlagadda Bardwell, designed the covers for this book manuscript. The background on the cover pages gives a Telugu (the language of my native tongue) translation of the book title (in the eyes of grandfather). My grandchildren gave me the inspiration and motivation in completing this manuscript.

Dr. Radha Krishna Rao Yarlagadda (2017)

Contents

Chapter One:
Family and Friends

Parenting:
1.1 Parents' Dedication

Mothers by nature are dedicated to taking care of their families. They are like a warm blanket to a child on a cold day. There is no other bond closer than the bond between a mother and her child. When a mother fixes toast, she takes the burnt pieces and gives the good pieces to her family. Father takes the end pieces. In families where there is very little food, children are fed first. Nature's mandate to parents is the survival of their children. Parents give unconditional love to their children! An old saying is, *"Children are love made visible."* If there is a break in an adult child-parent relation, the child is the usual cause, but not always. Chinese honor the parents of an individual who has earned distinction, as they had a role in his/her success. This recognition is well deserved.

1.2 Parents' Expectations of Their Children

Parents would like to see their children do better than they did in regard to the family happiness, finances, respect in the society, etc. If so, everybody will prosper and live happily ever after. Such prosperity cannot continue in real life. Consider the finances. If each generation in a family continues to prosper, then at the end of several generations they will have the wealth of the world. Children have the onus of family expectations to do well in life. There will always be successful and unsuccessful generations. If your children have done well, and are not dependent on the State, then you have succeeded. One of the Bible sayings is, "*Judge the tree based on its fruit.*"

If one of your children is a burden on the society, you have failed in some sense. To have successful children, parents need to have an active part in their lives. Children are not pets. They need constant attention. Let them make their own mistakes. If they are not physically hurting themselves, there is nothing wrong to let them make mistakes. They learn from their mistakes. It is part of growing up.

1.3 Parents' Concern for Their Children

Three generations (grandparents, parents and grandchildren) were living in the same house. The roof needed fixing. The son decided to fix the roof in the middle of the day. He was vigorous and could handle the hot sun. The grandfather saw his son working in the sun and was not happy. He asked his son to come down. The son said, "*Dad, I can handle it,*" and continued to work. The grandfather was not happy and brought his grandson outside. The father saw his young son under the hot sun and was upset. He came down from the roof and asked his father, "*Who in the world put my son under the hot sun?*" The grandfather nodded and said that, "*You are my son, no matter how old you are. It hurts me to see you under the hot sun. Please understand. Parents worry about their children until the end of their life. That is part of nature.* "

1.4 Train Your Young Children

You can bend a sapling and make a vine around a tree. You can train a child to get used to good habits, give respect to elders, and grow up to be a respectable adult. Help your children financially to achieve their goals. Make sure they understand the value of money. Help them to be effective in their education. You can train young children to your liking. Figuratively, you can train a child you can carry, whereas you cannot train an adult male child who can grow a beard. You cannot force any of your adult children to do something he or she does not want to do. Elizabeth G. Hainstock[5] suggests, "*Never do for a child what he is capable of doing himself.*" If you do, you are essentially training that child to be an invalid. Children have imagination. They lose that as they grow. Society thwarts their imagination instead of fostering their imagination.

Children learn better if you let them keep their own pace. Watch your children's activities and their friends. When peer pressure on your children exceeds family control, they may join wrong groups getting into trouble. S. Truett Cathy[6] has a nice saying, "*...You reap much more than you sow, just as a kernel of corn planted yields much more than a single kernel. Sow a seed of trouble, and you'd harvest a bushel of sorrow.*"

1.5 First Child

If a first child is successful, the chances are the other children will be, too. Young children tend to respect the oldest child, as they perceive them to be smarter and experienced. Parents want their first-born child to be successful so that the other children will follow. In most families, youngest child deviates more so from the family wishes.

1.6 Habits of Children

Spending habits, interests in food and music, political and religious convictions, and appreciation of education follow family traditions. Children have a stronger relationship with relatives from the mother's side of the family compared to the father's side of the family. Teenage and young adult children want to do the opposite of parent's desires. They rebel to show their independence. If there is enough love and direction in the family, children will follow the family traditions and appreciate the family discipline in later years. Every parent should learn from Dr. Sigmund Freud's[7] statement, "*It is not attention that child is seeking but love.*"

Children of religious people tend to be religious. Yet, at times, preacher's children rebel and have problems. Children of educated families tend to be educated.

Children are not prejudiced. Prejudice comes through learning from parents and surroundings. Helping children grow is like constructing a temple, adding a tile here and there, forming a mosaic of habits and convictions that follow the pattern of the parents and their mentors.

Children learn from their mistakes. It is a trial and error process. Parents can tell their own mistakes to their children and help them not to make similar mistakes. Mentoring young ones is important. Schools, universities, and other groups are there to reduce the time in learning process. Whether it is algebra, grammar, or any other subject, it is easier and takes less time to learn from teachers than learning by themselves.

1.7 Behavior Patterns of Children

A child thinks that his parents are great. A teenager thinks his parents are not very bright. Eventually, an adult child realizes how smart his parents are. Parents have not changed, but the child has progressed in life from childhood to teenage to adulthood.

We can predict the behavior patterns of children by observing their friends. If they are friends with losers, they will become losers. If they are friends with drug addicts, they will become drug addicts. You may not be able to break their habits or friends when they become teenagers. You need to train them when they are young. Expose them to many activities and encourage their interests. Find out what your children want to do and be. If you think that activity nurtures their abilities, encourage them to your fullest. Be a part of their activities by attending their functions. These activities could be sports, music, or any other extracurricular activity. Children watch their parents. If they sense their parent's support, they will respond in a positive way. Spending time with children is the most important contribution you can make to society.

If you are a model citizen, it does not mean that your children will be model citizens. However, in order for children to be model citizens, parents need to strive for their own best behavior. If parents smoke, drink, and expect their children to do otherwise is not going to work. Children look up to the parents first, and, then their older siblings. When the younger children do well in any endeavor, the older siblings will be proud of their younger siblings. Parents should spend enough time with their first born to start the proper direction, values, etc. so that the tradition carries on.

In strong families, a matriarch (or a patriarch) plays a significant role. In the older countries, these may be grandparents or great uncles. The uncles and aunts can play important roles, also. These days, with a changing world and ever-moving families, older family members have less influence on the younger ones.

1.8 Structured Activities of Children

Children like to have a structured life, as it allows them to make progress in life in a systematic manner. Parents should provide a framework for them to have a successful and enjoyable life. Teach them the importance of planning.

1.9 Do Not Forget Your Family Roots

Learn where you came from, how far you have progressed in life, and focus on where you want to go. Be true to yourself. Respect your heritage. Have respect for yourself. If you do not, nobody else is going to respect you.

1.10 Sayings on a Daughter and a Son

A daughter is your daughter as long as you live; a son is a son until he gets married. Most children look after their parents in their old age. It depends upon how the children were brought up and how their grandparents were treated in their times of need.

Throughout history, sons are the mother's favorites, and daughters are the father's favorites. Humans are more critical of their own kind, as they know what they had gone through as a family member to be successful in their life and, at the same time, helpful to the family. Also, opposites attract.

One of Robert Frost's[8] quotes is, *"The father is always a Republican toward his son, and his mother's always a Democrat."*

1.11 Losing a Child

Not being able to see your children is gut-wrenching. Young ones cannot understand it until they have their own children. Losing a child before a parent passes away is the worst pain and agony a parent could endure and have to get through.

1.12 Affection is Important to Children

Show affection to your children. When they did something wrong, show them their mistakes, and direct them in a positive way. Discipline your children with love.

1.13 Family Secrets

Keep your family secrets in the family. No one should air his or her dirty laundry. Bertrand Russell's[9] said, *"No one gossips about other people's secret virtues."*

1.14 Youngsters and Their Distractions

When kids listen to music doing their homework, their brain is doing two jobs. Children who can concentrate well in their studies were taught from the beginning to shut out any bad influences. Successful families make sure that their children learn how to concentrate by providing them a desk in their room and a door that they can close to concentrate on their work. These do well in life. Children who can concentrate tend to succeed with what they have. They know they are accountable for their actions.

1.15 Family Vacations

Family vacations need to be planned so that everyone in the family has a good time. Timing is important. Arrange sightseeing trips that have breaks and are enjoyable for the family. Carry a glass of crushed ice to chew when you are driving during long trips. This keeps one from falling asleep while driving.

Family vacations can be enjoyable learning processes. When we went to see the great Sequoias in California, I overheard teenagers conversing with their parents. The parents wanted them to enjoy the park with the trees that are of phenomenal in size and the majesty of Sequoias. The daughter said, "*If you see one tree, you have seen them all.*" Another one I heard was a boy from the same family making fun of an old man with deep wrinkles all over his face. The old man had experiences, both good and bad in his life. His face indicated that he went through troubles and tribulations. The comments by the teenagers indicated that they needed to grow up and mature.

Being a Grandparent:
1.16 Children and Grandparents

Children and grandparents are natural allies. Grandparents are our continuing tie to our near-past. If children treat their parents properly, grandchildren will appreciate the love of their grandparents, and understand their importance in the human chain.

1.17 Grandchildren

Grandchildren are precious. They are like interest on your bank accounts or dividends you get from your stock. You have the primary responsibility of your children and enjoyment of your grandchildren. As long as they are behaving properly, you can keep them; when they start acting up, you can send them back to their parents.

1.18 Doting Grandfathers

Grandfathers tend to be conservative in their behavior. They are very serious with their own children, but when it comes to their grandchildren, they are relaxed. Grandchildren are a joy. Don't compare your grandchildren, as each one is different.

Being a Spouse:
1.19 Features of Husbands and Wives
When a young man starts dating, without even thinking, he looks for girls with features similar to his mother and eventually selects a young woman that has similar features as his mother. It is common to hear many young men saying after few years of marriage they have married (a person similar to) their mother.

In countries where arranged marriages are prevalent, husband and wife's features are not similar like in the Western countries where they select their partners. Selection is complex in arranged marriages with relatives involved in the process. The wedding couples' features reflect the family spectrum in terms of size, shape, color, etc.

1.20 Old Sayings on a Husband and a Wife
Some of the old sayings came from habits from the previous centuries. The woman feels the house she and her husband lived in is hers. Courts in this country go with this logic during divorce proceedings. The husband feels that the house belongs to both. In the olden days, the woman stayed at home and the husband earned the income. The husband at work was away during the day and had to worry about his work and home. The wife took care of the home, but he was paying for it through his efforts and, therefore, both owned the house. A wife felt whatever the husband inherited and earned was theirs and the money she inherited from her family was hers. This came from the past when the inheritance was for the sons, and the daughters got their inheritance in the form of a dowry. In any argument with a wife, wife usually wins nine out of ten times. An old saying is, *"The rooster may crow, but the hen rules the roost."*

1.21 Losing a Wife or a Husband
If one of the couple is not interested in getting a divorce, but the spouse is, heartache persists and may not go away. If a spouse dies, there is a closure. Whereas in a divorce, there is a closure only in terms of law but not in heart or mind. There is a constant reminder if there are children involved. Couple would survive, but the children take a toll on their psyche. Both parents should attend to their children's needs.

1.22 Couples

Successful couples are in harmony like two wheels in a cart. They do not take anything for granted. Carts have an axle forcing the two wheels to function together. If one wheel goes faster than the other, the cart may even go in circles. Couples synchronize their thoughts and activities. They need to complement each other.

It is best to use solid information rather than using emotions in making any decisions. A successful couple consults with each other before making any major decision. They follow a smooth and a synchronized path. It is more likely that wife tries to find about her husband's side of the family history, as she is part of a new family.

1.23 Difficult Unions

We hear horror stories about young couples going through rough marriages. There are always two sides to any argument. Following are some.

"My spouse looks at what I do wrong and never says anything about the good things I do. Criticism and nagging is the trait. I never do anything right. My first wife always pointed out what I did wrong, whereas my second wife encourages me for all the good things I do." Living with these spouses is like day and night.

The signs of problems may or may not appear in the early stages of a marriage. Young couples are enamored in love and are not concerned about their future. Spousal abuse and dishonesty by a member of the couple leads to the breakup of a couple.

1.24 Too Many Divorces These Days

At least half of the marriages today end in divorce. Half of the surviving marriages may be together because of children, family pressures, finances, etc., indicating that three fourths of marriages may not be happy.

A marriage must be a happy union of two friends. No two individual minds can agree on every item. If there is true love, the couple will work out their differences, grow their relationship, never take their mates for granted, and they rely on each other.

1.25 Societal Levels of Husband and Wife

An old adage in India is husband and wife should come from about the same level in a society. If one person comes from a rich or a powerful family, or an educated family, and the other one comes from a poor or an ordinary family, or an uneducated family, there are going to be problems. People from rich and powerful families expect to be on a pedestal. A person coming from a workaholic family tends to be workaholic. In that situation, if one of the mates is from a relaxed family, he or she will become lonely.

Maintaining Good Relations:
1.26 Family Relations
Every family is different. Some children are happy by nature and others are not. Parents can be as happy as their unhappy child. When one of the children is in distress, every family member has the most sympathy for this child, sometimes even at the expense of other children. Parents and the older children carry the burden.

1.27 Your Family
You do not select your family. You inherit them. An old saying in India is, "*You do not poke your eye with your own finger.*" Be kind to your family members. Do not personalize your differences, especially political and religious differences. An old farmer is ill. His sons are feuding about the family property after their father's death. The farmer summons his sons to the bedside and asks them to bring several twigs from the back yard in a bundle. He asks each son to break the bundle. No one could break it. Then he asks each one to break a stick. Without any trouble, each son breaks a stick. He said, "*If all of you are together and support each other, outsiders cannot break our family. Unity is strength, whether it is a family, or a group, or a country. Strive for family unity!*"

1.28 Family Quarrels
Getting into the middle of a quarrel between spouses, siblings, etc. is tricky. If you do, both sides will criticize you. If the arguing pair is close, they will make up their differences. No one can be Solomon-like. It is better not to be part of a triangle.

1.29 Forgive and Make Up
In families there are going to be conflicts. Some make hurtful comments they really do not mean and may be hard to forget. Some keep the comments in front and keep them refreshed resulting in hatred, draining anyone's energy,

and the relations become strained. There is no end to this, unless the parties involved want to keep their enmity until death of one of the party members. The enmity tears all the family members apart. It is especially hard on the elders and children in the family. The following quote is from Life Application Bible, New International Version: 1 Corinthians13:4-5.

"Love is patient, love is kind. It does not envy, it does not boast, it is not proud. It is not rude, it is not self-seeking, it is not easily angered, it keeps no record of wrongs."

Communication, understanding and forgiveness are the components in any relationship. Resolve family conflicts within a reasonable time. No one can mediate until the parties wish to reconcile their relationships. Delaying will amplify the worst, as the relationship goes from affection-to-sadness-to-anger and to a point of no return. We have to accept that some adults may never reconcile. Time generally heals the wounds! In life, nothing gives more pleasure than replacing enmity with friendship.

1.30 Tough Love

These words are used when a parent or a mentor treats someone harshly with the intent of helping that individual. Tough love is hard on the parents. When the economy is good and the children are from a well-to-do family, parents tend to be lenient; without discipline, no one can succeed. Children think their life will be easy if there are no boundaries. With experience, they learn to like discipline and may not want to admit it. When children grow up and have their own children, they say they were glad for the discipline during their childhood. You cannot buy love from your children or anyone!

1.31 Perception in the Workplace

You are the boss of an organization and your close relative, Joe, is working in your organization. The employees' perception of Joe's contributions varies. If Joe is good, the employees treat him better than he deserves. If he is average, he gets what he deserves. If he is below par, the employees will treat Joe worse than he deserves.

1.32 Advice to Parents

Trying to resolve conflicts among adult children by parents can be treacherous and gut wrenching. Parents have a tendency to boss their adult children making the problem worse. Chances of resolving conflicts among children by parents are minimal and should be left to the siblings to resolve their conflicts. Many times the conflict is sharing of inheritance, which is easy to resolve, as the parents have the complete control of their property. You may think "*What do I care who gets what after I die.*" If parents do not do their part, it creates problems for the children, and the friction between them will last a long time and gets worse when the siblings have their own families.

1.33 Dealing with One That Hurt You

A friend or your colleague may not have been truthful with you. You might keep a grudge and cannot forget the harm done. Keeping grudges will slowly eat you like termites eating wood foundation in your house. The other person who hurt you may not even know it, and you are not helping yourself by stewing. What are you to do?

First, find out why he hurt you. Did he do it out of malice? Is he a pathological liar? Is this the first time, or is there a pattern of his behavior? He may want to be nice to you and will say anything to avoid any arguments, a weakness developed during his childhood. His family wanted him to be good, and he liked to please them. After he grew up, this behavior pattern continued. If the lies are due to a weakness, feel sorry for him and prepare for a repetition of the same behavior in the future. If someone acts with malice, break off any serious relationship with that individual. In an office environment, be civil. If there is physical violence, individuals may not be able to settle the conflict; professionals need to be involved. Consulting a counselor may help.

1.34 Do Not Bite the Hand That Feeds You

If you are doing well, remember the ones that helped you. This generation is doing better because of the previous generation's work. No one reaches the top of his profession without others' help. If you offend the person who helped you, he is not going to help you later. If one is doing something wrong, discuss with him in civil terms.

1.35 Progress in Life

In measuring your progress in life, do not compare yourself to others. Measure yourself with your own standards. By adhering to your own standards, you will be able to see how far you have come and what you need to do to achieve your goals. Focus on your goals. Optimism and power of positive thinking helps.

Face realities, as they are, not as you wish. Remember that winners write history and losers question why it happened.

When things are not going well, we wish otherwise. Such dreaming is understandable in the case of a bad marriage, a relationship, or in a job. Negative thinking does not help anyone. You cannot change anything that happened even a second ago, let alone a few days or years ago. If you have made a mistake, admit it. One of the worst things anyone can do is lie to you. Or, worse yet, is lying to yourself. A single lie destroys the integrity of the person who lied and any respect he had from others.

1.36 Clean Up Your Relationships

It is important to mend relationships with your immediate family, colleagues, or neighbors. If you have slighted someone, apologize as soon as possible. Reasonable people appreciate that. If someone slighted you, make sure that you are right and visit with the individual. If he or she is not interested in continuing any dialogue, do not associate with him or her, except in the case of a family member. In such a case, visit with a family member that has a good relationship with the other party and see anything can be done to mitigate the situation. Women are good at relationships.

People behave differently in a situation. Some are open and admit their misbehavior. Others show it by being overtly nice. Some cannot admit they are wrong and continue to be antagonistic. There is not much one can do with them. Consulting a counselor may help. Ruptured relations are harder to mend than strained ones. Remember the old saying, *"Trust and respect are necessary ingredients of a good relationship."*

1.37 Criticisms

Do not criticize someone unless you walked in that person's shoes. We criticize other parents because one of their children got into trouble, even though we do not know what the problem was. Could it be the child may have been mistreated when he was young or there is some genetic problem? Have the facts before making any comments.

Children observe their parents, relatives, and others respected by parents. Do not criticize your children for mistreating their pets or friends if you mistreat your spouse, children, and others. Do not tell children to clean up their rooms if you do not keep your home tidy. They are watching you. If you want them to be good, you should be the same. With children, use the words "*do the best possible*" instead of "*be perfect*." Be kind to the children and it is part of being parents. Even a little positive encouragement from a parent, a relative, a teacher, or by anyone gives a boost to the morale of a child.

1.38 Keep Yourself and Your Family Busy

With the advent of Internet, people are prone to being corrupted. Internet lures people and exposes them to things that are foreign to them that are both good and bad. Before Internet, people went to the cities to get exposure to bad and dangerous things. Help your children avoid experimenting bad and dangerous things by keeping them busy.

1.39 Sharing with Friends

An old saying is, "*A friend is someone that reaches for your hand and touches your heart.*" Sharing bad news with friends halves the ills; sharing good news doubles the happiness. Cooperation and sharing helps all involved.

1.40 Do Not Volunteer Anyone

We take our families for granted. For instance, your neighbor may ask if your son or daughter will do something while they are on a vacation. The tendency is to say, "Sure my son, daughter or spouse will do it." This creates havoc, as you are dictating to your family member. Volunteer someone only after you check with that individual.

1.41 Mental, Physical, and Family Strengths

Mental strength is the will and the determination of the person. The effect of physical strength without mental strength is minimal. Family strength gives one a good start in life.

1.42 Sour Relations

You have a friend, or a colleague. After each meeting you get depressed and feel that he uses you and treats others differently. What can you do? An old saying is, "*If a cold breeze is coming through your window, the thing to do is close the window.*" Cut your relationship with him or her. Everyone has the power to like or dislike someone. No one can force you to like or dislike someone.

1.43 Romantic Relations

Romantic relationships are hard to understand, as they are irrational. Always go into any permanent relationship with caution.

1.44 Parents Expect Their Children to Do Better

When children of unsuccessful parents fail, some say it is expected. Behavior patterns of children are similar to their parents. Parents want their children to have a better life than they have. Success or failure cannot continue from one generation to the next and to the next. If it continues, the growth will be exponential. This is against nature.

Parents tend to push their children to levels they are not capable of reaching. They can push a child to success only so far, as one can only push a child climbing a tree so far, unless the parents carry him (or her) to the top on their backs. Children have limitations. By pushing their children too much, parents might even hurt them. Most parents give about the same amount of help to all their children. Some children take advantage of it and succeed. Some realize they do not have what is required to achieve the goals set by others and choose to achieve them at their own level and pace. Some do not even realize they are incapable of achieving their own goals, strive with little successes, and are unhappy. All fruits do not mature at the same time. In the same vein, we can surmise that children mature at different times of their life.

Children who work with their parents or relatives tend to have a good future. They grow up to be well balanced and contribute to the society significantly. In these cases, no one should be surprised if a son (daughter) tells his father (mother) that "I am like you in so many ways" and thank the parents profusely when they are adults.

Most do not like to hear bad news. Fathers do not like to hear about the bad behavior of their children when they come home after work. Many comic shows use the line, *"Wait till your father comes home."* Father would rather love to hear the good news about his children, as it is a welcome relief after a hard day's work. Children are children. They act, behave, and learn in their own way. They do well if they are raised in a good family environment. Follow the advice of Nobel Laureate Rabindranath Tagore[10], *"Don't limit a child to your own learning, for he was born in another time."* Don't expect your children to behave the way you want them to behave, or like you were. If you were raised in a community with a different set of formalities and values than now, you have to learn and find the proper and best ways to raise your children.

1.45 Inheritance Traits

A child inherits some of the distinguishing qualities, and also some of the peculiarities, of the family. After all, a child gets his or her DNA from the family. An old Indian adage is that a girl's behavior resembles that of an aunt on the father's side, whereas a boy's behavior resembles that of an uncle on the mother's side.

1.46 Use Your Heart with Family and Friends

Trust between two people is sacred. Once it is broken, it is almost impossible to restore. When you are dealing with family, friends, and colleagues, and for that matter to anyone else, how and what you say and do is important. You may disagree with them, but always be respectful. The only ones you can hurt are the ones you love the most. When dealing with the ones you love write their good deeds on your heart and write their faults on the beach sand. If you use a microscope to analyze the actions of family and friends and expect perfection, you will be unhappy and cause your family and friends to be unhappy. You can expect unconditional support from your parents, as the support comes from their heart. Parents can never stop worrying about their children until they die!

One of Vauvenargues'[11] quotes is, *"Great thoughts spring from the heart."*

Chapter Two:
Make the Best of Your Life

Self-Survival:
2.1 Look after Yourself

No one can look after you better than you can. Even your mother cannot feed you unless you tell her that you are hungry. If you need a favor from someone, ask for it. Do not forget your roots, as they are your initial conditions. Your success or failure depends on how you work with what you have. Build a network that would be beneficial to you.

2.2 Confidence

Have confidence in your actions. A supervisor, a teacher or even a parent can destroy your confidence by criticizing you every time you fail. Encouragement and support develop confidence. Loss of self-confidence makes one impotent. Try to achieve short-term goals. Completing these will help you achieve long-term goals.

2.3 Do Things Based on Gut Feeling; Evaluate Before Doing

You have a hunch, and your thoughts are sketchy. Before you act, evaluate if your hunch is a wishful one. Is there a basis for your hunch? Look for consistency. Have a solid plan, evaluate, and execute. Perseverance prevails. Don't take shortcuts.

2.4 Peace with Yourself and Unfriendly Ones

When things are not going well, think about what the Persian King had carved on his ring, "*This, too, will pass.*" Try not to be critical of yourself and others. The biggest wounds are self-inflicted. Learn to be your own friend. If you cannot have peace with yourself, then you cannot have peace with others.

To change unfriendly ones to your side, tell them something they can cheer about themselves. They may not become your friends, but they will be amicable.

2.5 Do Not Burn Your Bridges after Crossing

You never know when you need someone's help. Be kind to everyone you come across. If you are changing your job, be on good terms especially with your co-workers and your supervisor. Your last employer is your best reference for your new job.

2.6 Actions Have Consequences

Use your words carefully. Say something only if you mean it. Otherwise, you lose credibility. If you get excited every time there is a problem, people will ignore you. Words and actions have consequences. One of the sayings of Muhammad is, "*Actions will be judged according to intentions.*"

2.7 Change before You Have To

If you are hanging onto a job that is not to your liking, find another job before your supervisor forces you to find another job. The same applies to a relationship. Change before you have to. Do not wait until it is too late. Face reality.

2.8 Learn from Your Failures

You learn more from failures than winnings. Do not gloat when you win. Learn about yourself and accept your limitations. Use your abilities and inner strength to achieve your goals.

2.9 Watch Your Energy Levels

If your energy level is too low, you may say or do something that you regret later. Before you talk or take action, think and have a plan. Check your energy level and your moods. Be on guard. It is easy to ruin a relationship or a friendship with snappy comments. Do things from your strength. Support from your family and friends will boost your energy level.

2.10 Use the Information You Have
Use all the available information to do good things for yourself and others. Do not worry about what happened in the past, except do not repeat past mistakes. Learn from your mistakes. Don't ask a question if you are not prepared for the worst answer!

2.11 Live Life for Yourself and Your Family
Be kind to yourself and your family. One of the quotes in *Talmud* is, "*The highest wisdom is kindness.*" Recognize what you are and not what you want to be. Help your family when needed. You will be unhappy if you behave according to others' reactions.

2.12 Simple Notes to Follow
Learn from the past. Live in the present. Plan, focus, and strive for the future. If you ignore the future, you have failed. The past is like looking in your rear view mirror while driving, as you cannot concentrate on what is ahead of you. Do not dwell on the past failures. Concentrate on the job at hand, and do your best. You will succeed.

Remember the old saying, "*Misery loves company and everyone involved will lose. Cheerful attitude and good planning bring happiness and successes.*" Everyone goes through anger. It will not solve any unless one directs it to get positive results. Successful ones use this approach, and losers use anger in a destructive way.

2.13 Opportunities
If you work hard, opportunities come in disguise and in a bunch. Recognize them and use them to achieve your goals. Make sure the opportunity is not one of your wishful dreams and you are on a strong footing. Make use of any opportunities you come across in life. We have a very short life on this Earth and have only a few opportunities to achieve our goals. Remember that, "*A missed opportunity is worse than a defeat.*"

2.14 Take Responsibility for Your Actions
You can measure the quality of a man if he takes responsibility for his actions.

Many take credit for their actions if all goes well and blame others if things go bad.

2.15 Do Not Gloat When You Win and Do Not Sulk When You Lose

If you gloat when you win, you are rubbing the other person's face into dirt. It may make you feel good for a few minutes. If you are gracious to your opponent, you may get his support and friendship in the future. You never know when you will need someone's help. When you lose and sulk, you are only hurting yourself. Analyze your loss, learn from your mistakes, be good to yourself and your friends, and move on.

Problems:

2.16 Recognition is the First Step in Curing Many Problems

The first step in understanding your problem is recognizing that you have one. Then understand the cause of it. Is this due to your actions or is it due to someone else's actions? Accepting the responsibility for a problem you caused goes a long way toward solving such a problem. Some are so stubborn and are not willing to give an inch. In such cases, there is no real solution. They are asking for bigger problems. Putting oneself in a box does not help anyone, including the one in the box. Success does not require any explanation and failure does not need an alibi. Do not blame others for your problems.

2.17 Handling Problems

If there is a personal problem, try to handle it yourself. Others have less of an interest in solving it. In case of knotty problems, get advice from your family and friends. One of Pres. Calvin Coolidge's[12] quotes is, *"The right thing to do never requires any subterfuge. It is always simple and direct."*

Material problems pale in comparison with personal problems. It is tempting to fix some equipment yourself that you are incapable of fixing. If so, get some professional help. It is cheaper in the end. Learn to accept your limitations!

2.18 Irritations

Kumaragiri Vema Reddy, respectfully known as Vemana, was a fourteenth century Telugu poet. He is considered as one of the best Telugu poets ever. His poems discuss wisdom, morality, and everyday life. The collection of his poems, called *Vemana Setakam*, is studied by children in Andhra Pradesh, India.

Charles Phillip Brown, an Englishman by descent, translated his poems into English with the title, *Verses of Vemana* in 1829.

One of the Vemana poems gives a list of irritations. Adding a few additions to his, they are, a piece of meat in your teeth, a fly in your eye, a bee buzzing near your ear, a pebble in your shoe, a tick inside your skin, a sliver in your hand, a burr on your saddle, a chirping cricket or a cicada in your home, conflicts at home, etc. Attend to them.

2.19 Minor Mistakes

Do not turn a minor mistake into a major one. Minor mistakes do not hurt anyone in the long run. Do not make a molehill into a mountain. Do not use an axe if you can do a job with a needle. Be kind to yourself and others, especially to the ones who made mistakes.

2.20 Major Mistakes

One of the worst mistakes one can make is hate someone, including self. Arthur Schopenhauer states the origins of hate and contempt are as, "*Hatred comes from heart; contempt, from the head.*" Hermann Hesse[13], a Nobel Laureate, puts it succinctly that, "*If you hate a person, you hate something that is part of yourself. What isn't part of ourselves doesn't disturb us.*" Hate and contempt are self-inflicted and they hurt the individual if he or she cannot get over them. It hurts everyone involved, especially if one's family is involved.

2.21 Take a Small Step Each Time in Attempting to Solve Problems

Divide a problem into parts. No one eats the whole meal in one swallow. You eat one spoon at a time. You walk one step at a time. It is better to carry two small suitcases rather than one big one. Carrying a large suitcase breaks one's back. Have a good mental attitude. In any negotiation, you may not agree with a total package one side proposes. Consider one item at a time and put together a package that works. Do not get your ego dictate your decisions.

2.22 Be Flexible

Flexibility is a necessity in any relationship and in your plans. In life, you have to compromise. It is good to be proactive than reactive in any relationship. Rigidity results in breaks in relations. "Give and take" should be a motto for everyone. The one who looks at things like black and white has a simple decision, one or the other. In life, we have several possibilities to choose. Concentrate on the ones that you are satisfied with that have the highest probability of success and do them.

2.23 Do Not Lose Hope

One may be a homemaker, a sales clerk, a student, an employee, or whatever. There will be times one feels helpless, wanting to give up or, using the colloquial language, *"throw in the towel."* For a cook, the next meal stares in the face. It seems there is no end. Wash clothes and the next pile is there. Clean your house, and the next day it needs cleaning again. You feel like giving up. Use a plan and assign your family members certain chores. Make them feel that as part of the family; they are doing chores that are necessary. Multiple hands make the routine work tolerable. Have several rooms to clean, just clean one room at a time. After finishing the first room, go to the next. Take one step at a time and you will get your job done.

A student (or an employee) may have assignments to complete from time to time. The one who plans his work systematically is efficient. He does a better job than the one who frets and tries to complete his work at the last minute. One never knows about any unseen problems, such as illness or other unpredictable problems. Give yourself time to complete your work. Enjoy when you complete your work successfully.

2.24 Whatever You Look For, You Will Find It

Successful individuals find opportunities in the midst of adversities. Losers look for doom and gloom. I heard a story of a young man passing through a small town in Oklahoma who stopped at a gas station. The owner of the station was an old man with a wrinkled face. The young man said that he was looking for a town to live in and asked the old man the question, *"Are the people in this town nice?"* The old man asked the young man, *"Are the people in the town you are from nice?"* The young man said they are all snobs, and he did not like them. The old man said, *"The people in this town are just like the people you have dealt with before, and they are also snobs."* The young man did not understand, and asked the old man, *"How could that be?"* The old man replied

"People are the same everywhere, whether they are from your town or anywhere."

In life, you will find what you are looking for. In the Old West movies, many young men thought that they were the best gunslingers. Most of them died during their first encounter. If you look for prosperity, you will find it. If you look for wisdom, you will find it. If you look for goodness in people, you will find it. If you look for negatives in people, you will find them. If you are good to your family, friends and neighbors, they will be good to you. Human relationship is a bilateral relationship.

2.25 Instant Gratification

We want to do everything quickly with instantaneous gratification. Anyone expecting to benefit without working hard is a gambler and will not succeed in the end. Long-term growth is better than short-term benefits.

Economy:

2.26 Investments

Stockbrokers and pundits in the economic field tell everyone to diversify their investments. If one company is not doing well, some of the other companies we invested in may help us average the income better.

It is hard to keep track of stocks for us laymen, as we do not know the decision makers and how they make them in a company located faraway. If we invest in our own community, we can react quickly. Diversifying your activities and getting income from several sources minimizes your risk. An old saying is, *"No risk, no glory!"*

2.27 Learn About the Knowledge Economy

Learning the knowledge economy essentially uses one's intelligence to make money. Today's economy helps one from a rich family. He has a cushion to fall back on. He may not use his family's wealth; or, he may not even need it. Having it gives him name recognition to boost to his status. It also gives him false confidence and, in some cases, may adversely affect his future. Historically, many of the sons and daughters of rich people with old money became politicians and contributed to the society.

There are many who come up to be outstanding politicians with humble beginnings and have done equally well. Many of them became CEOs of major companies. Society generally tends to be more critical of them if they make mistakes. If they do not, they get higher glory compared to the successful ones that used family wealth or stature. It is better to be successful on your own first. Use of knowledge economy is good. It would even catapult anyone to be wealthy and prosperous. Some politicians want to be elected to positions to have inside information on economy to help them financially. They even use propaganda, i.e., distorting the truth to achieve their goals. Successful ones control the events, rather than events control them!

2.28 Power, Money, and Talents

If you do not use money, power and talents for good causes, it is like not having any of these. Use your assets, including your senses, in achieving your goals. George Bernard Shaw[14] stated, *"Only those who have helped themselves know how to help others, and to respect their right to help themselves."*

2.29 Nothing is Black and White

In life, everyone has to make choices from a set of options. In simple terms, it is like a fork in the road you come to, and you do not know which way to go. There are three choices: first, go to the left; second, go to the right; and third, go to the middle, which will not go anywhere. Obvious choice is to pick either the left or the right. Assign penalties for one direction or the other and make a choice that minimizes the penalties in some form. Success belongs to the ones that made good choices in their life. If one cannot make a prudent decision, it would be wise to visit with a wise mentor.

Organization:
2.30 Clean Your Mind, Desk, Home, Etc., Regularly

Most people do not like cleaning. If you ask why, they say that things get messy or dirty in no time, so why clean. Have a schedule to clean at fixed intervals. Before leaving office, take care of papers that needed attention. Clean up your desk, files, papers, etc., even if you have the queasy feeling that if you throw away a paper, you may need later. If you get a letter, respond on the same day. If not important, throw it away. If you are looking for a paper on your desk, look systematically rather than haphazardly. Do not give any important papers to a person with a cluttered desk.

Many times we have items that are not used for a long time. They are lying on our desks or in our houses. Use the principle that if you have not used an item for a couple of years, it is probably not worth keeping. If the item has value, donate it to charity. Papers and papers, we are inundated by them. We were given a birth certificate when we were born and a death certificate when we die. We have to keep track of papers for taxes and the list goes on and on. Before going to bed, take care of the papers. File them if they are for information and pay the bills before they are due. Get into a routine. You may be frustrated by the routine in the beginning, but you will be happy in coming days, weeks, and years that you are on top of taking care of papers. Taking care of the routine items before going to bed allows for a fresh start in the morning. You are at ease to tackle the new items that need to be taken care of the next day. Doing it on a regular basis makes it easier on anyone's nerves!

2.31 Cleaning in Stages or a Total Clean Up

Some children rebel in cleaning their rooms. When you ask them to clean their rooms, they literally want to tear up their rooms and rearrange everything. This is one form of a rebellion of not wanting to do cleaning. If they do the cleaning in portions at a time, it gets easy. It is up to the parents to instill this notion in their children. Whatever you do, don't do the cleaning for them. If you do, you are essentially making them lazy and they would not do any cleaning in the future. Start training your children at an early age to keep their rooms neat. When children get used to the habit of keeping their rooms neat and clean, they will be proud of their room.

2.32 Number of Items in Mind

Minimize the number of items in your mind. Concentrate on one item at a time. Some you can put aside and consider them when they need attention. If you are working on a computer, and you have too much material in storage, it slows and may even die. Human minds are complicated and hard to understand. They are like computers that can store an incredible amount of material. Clean up your mind periodically. Take a vacation and recharge your batteries. When a job is finished, put it away from your mind, relax for an evening, and focus on your next day's work. If you failed to succeed in finishing your job, find out why you could not. Get some help next day. Have a file and document your work, especially the failures. Writing always helps to see why you have failed.

2.33 To Achieve a Goal

Plan in minute detail and have a burning desire to achieve a goal. Keep the desire in front of you. Visualize your dreams. It gives you a boost in achieving your goals. Planning without a burning desire is like having diffused sunlight.

If you focus the sunlight on an object long enough, you can burn a hole in it. One quote of Napoleon Hill's[15] is, "*Whatever the mind can conceive and believe, the mind can achieve.*"

Planning, discipline, and visualization help you achieve your goals. If you cannot see a path for success, make alternate plans. With practice and proper planning, you will achieve your goals. One of Thomas A. Edison's quotes is, "*Vision without execution is hallucination.*" If you do not have a definite plan and fortitude to complete a job, do not start.

Personal Attitude:
2.34 Attitudes Play a Major Role in Life
An old Quaker saying is, "*Attitudes are caught, not taught.*" If you have a good attitude in life, you can cope with many problems. The ones with bad attitudes are unhappy. They are a burden on everyone they are associated with. They expect sympathy.

I was taking a walk in our neighborhood. An elderly man and his wife were painting inside a new house being built. I complimented him for his hard work and told him that the house looks nice. At my first meeting with the couple, the man said that he was seventy-eight and his wife was seventy-two. He said that he has lived in more than ten different houses and built every one. I said you must be in good health to do all that work. He said, "*I have aches and pains like many elderly. Instead of complaining, I would rather work to keep me busy. Furthermore, complainers tend to be selfish, unhappy and inefficient. When I built my first house, I asked a painter for an estimate. The estimate was several thousand dollars. I did not have that kind of money, but had the time. On my own time, I painted the house. It was hard in the beginning, but once I got the knack of it, I could do a good job. I may not be able to do a job better than a painter can, but I can do a better job than the painter's hired hand. Learning what we can and cannot do is important. The ones I cannot do, I will find someone capable to do. I get enjoyment from simple successes in life.*" You cannot change your DNA, but you can change your attitude on life. Life is what you make out of it!

2.35 Personal Problems in the New World
Not too many people are interested in hearing your problems. Everyone is busy. When you tell an acquaintance that you are having problems, he will listen to you. He will be sympathetic and tell you that he will be available for

any help. When you tell him the next time, you will see that he is not interested, as he has his own problems.

Whom do you turn to? You may get sympathy from your family, friends, a spiritual leader, or a psychiatrist. We are now living in the stressful world. Working long hours is almost a necessity to progress in his or her profession. It takes a toll on the personal problems, especially on the psyche and on the family relations. Attending to the personal problems should be a top priority. Consulting a counselor should be encouraged when appropriate. It would make a world of difference.

2.36 Do Not Feel Sorry For Yourself

If you hurt one of your family or a friend, admit and apologize. It is better to admit your mistakes rather than others forcing you to admit. If you are sincere, your family and friends will understand you and plan to correct our mistakes. Based on your actions they will react. If you feel sorry for yourself, that will lead you nowhere. Everyone makes mistakes. If you made a mistake, accept it, and do not berate yourself. If your best friend made a mistake, you would not go on a tirade. Treat yourself as you treat your best friend. When someone is rude to you or accuses you, ask him to explain. In most cases, he will be conciliatory. Ignoring him encourages him to repeat. If he doubles down, you may have to standup for your rights.

2.37 Good and Bad Habits

Habits are learned. One can learn to be happy or sad. The ones with a cheerful outlook tend to live longer. They make others happy. The ones that look at the dark side of the world are unhappy and make the ones around them unhappy. Times change, but habits do not. Good habits are hard to acquire and easy to break. Learning good habits is like going against the wind or floating upstream in a river. It takes time and a constant effort to get into good habits. Avoid alcohol, illicit drugs, cigarettes and other habit forming items that can destroy you.

One of Benjamin Franklin's[16] quotes in his recently republished autobiography (Barnes & Noble, 1994) is, *"Tis easier to prevent bad habits than to break them."* Bad habits are self-destructive. The key is first consciously recognizing the bad habit, controlling it, breaking it, and finally changing the negative habit to a positive habit.

It is good to examine one's life from time-to- time and to improve one's habits and attitudes that to be better in dealing with others, to be happy and content. Winston Churchill[17] has a nice saying, *"We make a living by what we get, we make a life by what we give."* Benjamin Franklin[18] identifies several virtues (or good habits) to follow. Practicing good habits through frequent repetition, one-at-a-time, until each one becomes one's second nature is the best avenue to go through. A good motto for young ones is, *"Adopt and change for a better future."* Two of the best phrases in the English language are *"I am sorry"* and *"thank you."* Use these phrases whenever appropriate.

Chapter Three

Dealing with Others

Friends and Acquaintances:
3.1 A True Friend

A true friend is honest with you. He tells you when you are wrong, supports you when you need help, and compliments you when you have done well. Instead of telling you what you want to hear, he gives his best advice. If you need help, your friend will be there. Friendship is a two-way relationship. Most have only two or three "*true*" friends.

You select your own friends, whereas you inherit family members. If you have a good family, the family members care for you. They are your best friends; you can rely on them. Do not mistake acquaintances as friends, as the relationships are shallow.

3.2 Making Friends in Your Organization

It is not a good idea to be family friends with associates in your organization. Do not open your heart to individuals in your organization, as you are in competition with them. Be cordial with your colleagues. Be helpful whenever possible. If your colleague has to choose between you and him, it will be him.

3.3 Expecting Help from Friends and Family

Benjamin Franklin in his Autobiography nicely states, "*He that has once done you a kindness will be more ready to do you another than he whom you yourself have obliged.*" Children get help from parents, whereas the other way is not always the case. An older sibling is more helpful to a younger sibling than the other way. The employer and the employee relationship may be different, as both parties need to help each other in their professional growth. Helping your family and friends in need and the helpless is good for your soul. Asking for help is not a sign of weakness!

3.4 If You Want Someone to Help, Give Him Incentives

A parent is eager to help if his child is responsible in his actions. A friend will help you if he knows that you will stand by him when he needs help. An acquaintance will help you if he can expect help from you in the future.

Your supervisor will help you if you can help him to achieve his goals. A subordinate will help the supervisor if he knows that he can get raises and/or recognition. If you help someone, do not expect any returns from that individual.

3.5 Making Others Happy

If you want to make a person happy, find what makes him happy. To make the parents happy, help their children. To make your supervisor happy, do things that make him look good. To make your teacher happy, do your best in his class by making him proud of you. Medical doctors are admired, as their goal is the health and welfare of their patients. Caregivers help the sick and old to live at some comfort level. They are like angels. Making everyone happy is an impossible task. If that is your wish, you will be miserable. Decide who is dear to you and try to make them happy. Fewer the people you want to make happy, the better off you are.

3.6 Constructive and Destructive Relationships

It takes effort to have good relationships, such as in marriage, friendship, business partnerships, etc. It takes a silly word or a misstep by an individual to destroy a long relationship just as you can spoil milk by a drop of lemon juice. There is no way to recover the original milk. Similarly, if you destroy a relationship in the form of a gouge on the psyche, it is very difficult, often impossible, to repair it. Anger plays a major role in a destructive relationship. Siddhartha Gautama, the Great Gautama Buddha enlightened us that *"Holding on to anger is like grasping a hot coal with the intent of throwing it at someone else; you are the one who gets burned."*

It is easy to get into a relationship and painful to get out of a relationship. Human relationships are difficult and need to be handled with care, caution, and understanding.

3.7 Building Relationships

Before you build a strong relationship, find out what the other person expects of you and his or her rules of operation. Each has to respect the other's rules. Do not expect that everyone shares your feelings and behave to your liking. If you want to build a good relationship, accept the individual as he or she is. Many young married ones expect (or wish) to change the other person to their way of thinking. People do not change, unless they have gone through some traumatic experience and/or psychological counseling.

Words convey what the person wants to say. Words can cut like a knife. If you slip your tongue, you cannot take it back. If you slip your foot, you can recover. You learn more by using your ear than your mouth. Talk only if you have something to contribute. The ones that think before talking have respect. Treat others the way you want to be treated. Be kind. One of the rabbinical writings in Talmud is, *"Deeds of kindness are equal in weight to all the commandments."*

3.8 Relationships: Repair Them When Needed

Close relationships are like old socks. If you do not repair the holes in old socks, they get bigger. Some throw them away. Similarly, some discard their mates and friends when they see a problem. Keep up the relationships and repair any damages. You know the problems in an old relationship and may not know what the problems will be in a new relationship. There are others that have psychological problems and are not willing to get help. Some of these relationships may not be repairable. If they are physically sick, you can take them to a doctor. If they are mentally sick, they cannot help themselves. If one of the family members has psychological problems, living with him/her is like living in hell. One cannot force one to get help unless that individual is hurting someone, including himself/herself. In the case of physical and mental abuses, breaking the relationships may be inevitable and the best thing for all concerned, especially for the abused.

Remember that relationships require constant attention. If you do not, they are hard on your psyche and tough to repair any damages that are caused by your behavior.

3.9 Associations

If you associate with someone, you will acquire some of that person's character. Shady characters tend to be opaque and operate on the borderline. They are a bad influence on anyone. Avoid the shady characters. Coach John Wooden's[19] advice is, *"Be more concerned with your character than your reputation, because your character is what you really are, while your reputation is merely what others think you are."*

A friend with small children had a plan. He wanted them to associate with children of strict families. He made efforts to foster the associations. This will work only if started when the children are very young. It is too late if the children are teenagers. James Russell Lowell[20] suggests, *"A man's mind is known by the company it keeps."*

3.10 Arguments with Associates and Subordinates

Never get into a spitting contest with a skunk. Do not wrestle with a greased pig. Do not argue with a total loser. Your associates may have slighted you. If your co-worker is not doing his part, find the reason and let your supervisor know. It is easy to be angry or even lash out at someone. Control this behavior before landing yourself in trouble.

3.11 Good Rules to Follow in Arguments

In any argument or discussion, do not make things personal, as you lose your perspective. Keep things professional. When one loses control of himself in an argument, he loses. One remembers only the last outburst and forgets about how and what caused the argument. Honesty can be incredibly messy. Soft talk with logic always trumps. Some are good in making good arguments and others are good at taking them apart.

Diplomacy is the best approach. Mr. Dale Carnegie[21] championed that, *"To influence others to act, you must first connect to a core desire within them. This is a universal truth whether you are dealing with children or clients or (even) calves."*

If someone does not like to look at another point of view on a certain topic, he made up his mind. There is no use to discuss with this individual on that topic.

3.12 Taking Sides in an Argument

If you take one side in an argument, you are going to make one of the parties unhappy. Do not take sides in a family quarrel. In a professional arena, if you take one side, the other side will never forgive you. When you take a side, be on a solid ground. Find a common ground between parties and help them see it. They will respect you.

Tricky supervisors and some associates pit one person against the other. They want to be a referee, an arbiter and be above all concerned. Be careful with them!

3.13 Both Sides of an Argument

Some look at both sides of an argument. They are reasonable and compassionate. Some look at only their side. It is their way or the highway. These people are hard to deal with. Be careful in associating with them. Right-wing conservatives and left-wing liberals know what is right for everyone. Their life is simple. They make others' lives difficult.

3.14 Arguments and Stages of No Return

Every individual has frustrations and gets into arguments with others. Some arguments may go so far that normal relationships may not exist in the future, like spoiled milk. However, humans are resilient. When there is a break down in a relationship and a possibility for normalization, keep visiting after you simmer down. It is easier to push a moving object than a stationary object. Follow Pres. John F. Kennedy's[22] suggestion, *Never get in anything so deep that you've lost all chance of conciliation."*

3.15 Criticizers Are the First to Criticize Others

Criticizers cannot take criticism. Some can turn any argument around to blame others for their own mistakes. Watch your steps and document your moves in dealing with these. Disassociate with such people. Remember one of the old idioms, *"People who live in glass houses should not throw stones,"* as we all have faults and weaknesses. Others can hurt us by throwing stones at us.

3.16 Pointing Fingers at Others

Before you point fingers at others, note that there are four fingers pointing at you. Make sure that you are right before you accuse someone. You may not have made a particular mistake, but you may have contributed some to the other person's mistake through a misunderstanding. Be careful in pointing fingers at the other person, even when you are right. Be gentle. You may need help from the other person in the future. Be tolerant of others, especially the weak. In some sense, everyone is weak and make mistakes in different situations. Voltaire[23] philosophically stated the following: *"What is toleration? It is the prerogative of humanity. We are all steeped in weaknesses and errors: Let us forgive one another's follies, it is the first law of nature."*

3.17 Arguments and Misunderstandings

If someone takes a potshot at you, do not take it personally. He may have had a bad day, or he may not be feeling well. Find the reasons for his actions. Do not take anything personal, and you will have less stress and a better attitude in your life.

In life, there will be misunderstandings. Talk about who is right or who is wrong, rather than who is good or who is bad. Attorneys generally do not have a good reputation in society. I always wondered how opposing lawyers could even speak to each other after a bitter trial. They focus on their side of the arguments and not on the opposing attorney. They train themselves not to take the arguments personal.

3.18 Dealing with Ones Who Have Nothing to Lose

Losers are a drain to any organization. They generally have a bad record as long as a giraffe's neck. If you are in charge of them, put them in activities that do not affect the goals of your organization. Start a file on their ineffectiveness. One of the Polish sayings is, *"If you want to beat a dog, you can always find a stick."* Get rid of the losers before they drag your organization down.

Another group may include drug addicts. They will do whatever is necessary to get the drugs. Avoid them. If the drug addict happens to be one of your close relatives, or a friend, get him professional help.

Behaviors:
3.19 Quality of an Individual

Anyone can be magnanimous when things are going right. The character of an individual depends on how he reacts to adversities. Other measures include how he treats the ones working for him and how he reacts to the ones above him.

A quality individual is fair to all. He does not fix something that is not broken. He keeps old successful ideas and discards the ideas that are not. He does not change for the sake of change. Building a good reputation and goodwill takes a long time. It takes a short time to ruin the reputation built over a lifetime.

If you are looking for a good manager, look for a tough-minded but a fair individual to implement your plans. The *"goody, goody two shoes"* type is neither good for the organization nor to the employees he will be serving with or overseeing.

3.20 Personality of an Individual

The house (or office) a person occupies reflects his personality. The ones who own antiques or miscellaneous items have a hard time parting with most things. They keep the material things, whether needed tomorrow or twenty years from now or not.

Organized ones have their houses neat and well organized. The clothes are neat and pressed, and their shoes are polished. Bookcases are in order. If you drop in unannounced to their homes, they will apologize for their messy houses. It makes you feel that you are intruding. If you go to a person's house crammed with everything, you may feel uncomfortable, but the host makes you at ease.

There are others who like to keep everything organized but may not have energy or determination to keep everything neat. They tend to be edgy and they make the visitors uncomfortable. Never drop in to visit their home. Always, call before you visit. They have very few visitors at their homes.

Arnold J. Toynbee[24] puts it, *"One's actual temperament… is the foundation of one's personality."*

3.21 Behavior Patterns of Individuals

Behavior patterns of people do not change much from their past. Their behavior depends upon their initial conditions, how they grew up, their attitudes, and their desires. Each reacts differently in situations. We hire people by looking at their resumes. The history of an individual provides an indication of his future successes and possible failures. Professionals from good organizations tend to be successful, as they have seen success and yearn for such successes. Hard workers are always in high demand. One of the old sayings is, *"If you need something to be done, give it to a busy individual."*

Behavioral patterns can change if they go through a cataclysmic event or counseling. If not, liars will continue to be liars, cheaters will continue to be cheaters, philanderers will continue to be philanderers, backstabbers will continue to be backstabbers, lazy ones will continue to be lazy, whiners will continue to be whiners, and aggressive ones will continue to be aggressive. Narcissists do not show any remorse. If you condone bad behavior, you will get more of it. Abnormal behavior of individuals is due to unnatural hard-wired connections in their brains! Even though the brain is a learning machine, its hard-wire connections can only be changed physically. Some individuals want to be the center of attention and like to *"hold court."* Some exhibit their emotions outwardly and can be explosive. Stoic ones do not show emotions.

Initial conditions start with the genes and the family life. Our behavior also depends on the circles we spend time and live in. I was getting a hamburger. A Chinese father was ordering for his family's dinner. The person behind the counter could not understand his accent. His son came to the rescue. It does not matter how many years a person lives in a foreign country, he or she will not be able to pick pronunciation of the local dialect, whereas a child born to immigrants will talk and acts like one of the locals. On the other hand, with training, a professional singer from any part of the world can sing like a native. Immigrants, by necessity, need to adapt to new environments.

3.22 Behavior Patterns of Generations

People's behavioral patterns result from their family DNA, and the financial and social climate at the time of their youth. For example, the Builder generations in this country, i.e., the people who were born during the period 1928 to 1944, and the Baby Boomer generation born during 1945 to 1962 have different styles, attitudes, and behavioral patterns. The Second World War may have had some effect on these.

Builder generation grew up around the Depression years and money was scarce at the time. They tend to be savers and are concerned about their future. Most of them are high-school educated and few went to college.

Baby Boomer generation did not experience any struggles and are free-spirited. Their parents did not have enough money themselves to enjoy during their time of growing up, and they over-compensated their children by providing more than what is needed. Many of these are college educated compared to the previous generation. They tend to spend more money than their parents do. The free-spiritedness of the Baby Boomer generation brought the drug problem. In addition, the new gadgets changed the way the generations behaved. Builders balanced their checkbooks by hand and checked with their calculators. Today, Baby Boomers balance them by calculators and check them using paper and pencil. A small segment of the Baby Boomer generation built their wealth using the cyclical economy patterns, but the economy cannot continue to boom forever. There will be cycles of boom and bust, and life goes on.

3.23 Some Cannot See Others Succeed

Success is relative. Some succeed by working hard, and others succeed by being lucky. Luck favors the ones that are dedicated to their causes. Most people are fair and want their friends to succeed. Some want others to fail. They have principles that are lower than a snake's belly. The following Indian saying describes such ones. A person is praying and a genie appears before him and asks him, *"What would you like to have?"* She also says, *"You will get what you want and your associate (or your neighbor) will get twice what you get."* The man thinks it over and says to the genie, *"Blind me in one of my eyes."* Some get enjoyment when they see others in trouble.

3.24 People's Interests

Being born on the Indian subcontinent and working with students from all over the world, I had the privilege to interact with others from different cultures. All want a happy family. They want their children to be healthy and do better than they did.

Individuals from poor countries want to go to rich countries. Rich countries provide the necessities to the needy. Giving a free ticket to do what someone wants may make the individual a drag on the society. It is a delicate balance to do what is right.

There is corruption everywhere. In poor countries, some politicians are overtly corrupt, whereas in rich countries, they are covertly corrupt.

3.25 Judging a Group, Society, or a Country

You can judge a society based upon how it treats its young, old, and the helpless. Good societies take care of them. They pay their teachers well and respect them. The future of a society depends on the children. If we do not train the young ones, it is hard to change them later. Early education requires a good foundation and young ones can build their fortunes on that. We cannot build a skyscraper or even a small house without a good foundation. Without a good education, young ones will be destined to work in the service industry rather than being society leaders.

3.26 Group Control

Every group wants to set boundaries on its members' behavior. If the members follow the rules of the group, it provides them comfort, safety, and even funds etc. The less sophisticated the group is, the more stringent the requirements are on the members. Some even want their members to sacrifice their lives for their group. To achieve their goals, they even suppress the intellectual growth of their members. If the group is educated, its members tend to be independent. They will not sacrifice for the group.

3.27 People Are Different

Life would be dull if all the people were the same or even similar. If several people would like to marry the same person, there would be chaos. Diversity is nature's way of saying it is the best. Embrace it; benefit by it; and enjoy.

We inherit talents. We succeed or fail depends on how we use our talents. Good people see goodness in people, whereas cynics never see this and are unhappy.

3.28 Judgmental People

Judgmental ones have an opinion on most things and are hard to get along with. They look at everything in black and white. If an idea does not fit their interest, they consider it wrong. Their lives tend to be easier as they consider their side is right and the other side is wrong. Most assume religious people are tolerant. Some religious groups want to have their way or the highway in life. If you do not believe in their thinking, they consider you an infidel. Most conflicts are due to religious differences. Religion should be a calming factor. Religious zealots make everyone's life uncomfortable. Rebels and gangs are organized top-down rather than bottom-up like any civilized society. Cult leaders force their followers to be their slaves in body and spirit.

Nonjudgmental ones are easy to get along with. They look at all aspects of a situation. Unfortunately, some people label them as the ones without a backbone.

Personal Aspects:
3.29 If You Kill the Spirit of a Person, You Kill His Soul
Our goal should be to lift the spirits of others. If someone kills the spirit of an individual, that person becomes helpless and needs a boost in morale, which can come from a friend or even a stranger. One may think that lifting the spirit should come from clergy, social workers, psychiatrists, etc. Everyone should try to lift someone's spirit. A simple compliment from an individual to another one enhances the spirits of both.

3.30 Compartment-wise Personalities
There are many with split personalities. They cannot help themselves. Extreme ones may have a good family on one side and may be murderers on the other side. Most gangsters have nice families; however, they are ruthless in annihilating their opponents.

3.31 Verbal and Physical Abusers
Abusers exist in every culture. Animals do not kill other animals, except for food to survive. Sub-humans kill and hurt people and animals without a good reason. Physical abuses by men to women are more common than the other way around since men are physically stronger than women are. Verbal abuse can be subtle. If you confront the verbal abuser, he or she will say, *"Can't you take a joke?"* Sarcasm is meanness disguised in humor! Verbal abusers thrive on dialogues. They continue with their behavior when good people are silent on their behavior. Bullies respond to only strong directives and actions from authorities.

Abusers learned their behavior from their parents or from the society they live in. They are clever and polite before they abuse. They make you feel that you are going to lose their relationship if you confront them. Confront them. Tell them not to be abusive. If there is no progress, break the relationship.

3.32 Trusting Others
Most people are good hearted. There are always bad ones, however, and that is a part of nature. Use your experiences to determine the trusted ones. In either personal or professional relationships, be skeptical and verify, but not cynical. Cynical ones are unhappy in life. If you trust everyone you meet, you are living in an unreal world.

3.33 Successful Ones Have Self Control and Know Who to Deal with

Successful ones have the talent to control their mouths and their private parts. They can persevere and succeed in difficult situations. They can think fast and take action. They trust the ones who helped them before. If they see that the situation is not working to their advantage, they quickly change and start anew.

3.34 Liars

Liars have a mental problem. A single lie can destroy one's credibility. If a liar is an administrator, he loses all the respect of his supervisors and the ones he works with. The organization will go downhill. That is the time for him to step down. If he does not step down, his plans, his vision and decisions have no real meaning to the ones in the organization. Liars tend to be *"yes people."* They are looking after themselves, not the organization, or his associates. Never trust a pathological liar!

Lord Byron[25] states, *"One lies more to one's self than to anyone else."*

3.35 Politics, Religion, and Money

Human politics is an important part of life. An old saying is, *"Politics is a blood sport and is personal."* The two topics that invoke intense arguments are politics and religion, as they are emotional. Religious zealots and politicians like to convert everyone to their side, as they want them to follow their logic. Religion deals with the supernatural. No one can prove or disprove religious beliefs. Either you believe them, or you do not. In science, we say an experiment is valid if it is repeatable. Many argue that they can prove their beliefs from the documents that they have discovered. No one can prove the words are factual, as they are interpretations. Meanings of words change from time to time and certainly from previous centuries to today. Religion, in the name of God, has destroyed many lives and nations. If someone says that his religion is better than the others, he is saying that his beliefs are better. That is control. Conflicts are bound to appear. Politicians want to convince their electorate that their plans are the best.

Some argue that money, not religion, is the main culprit of disagreements. In the past, conquerors brought their religion into their newly conquered country and used their money and power to convert many of the citizens to their religion. It is easier to convert an uneducated, poor peasant than an educated or a well-to-do one. Money controls.

Some say, *"Politicians are crooked as a dog's hind leg."* Politicians tend to be orators stirring up emotions, giving ambiguous answers like the Delphic oracle, and have the charisma to convince people that their ideas are the best for the people they represent. Politicians like to convert people to their point of view. Politics is about future, not the past. Honest politicians are few and far between in this world!

3.36 A Letter Is More Effective Than a Telephone Call

Whether it is personal or professional, a letter requires a lot of thought if written properly. A telephone call or an oral conversation does not take much effort. E-mail is somewhere between a letter and a telephone call. It is not effective, either. They are fast and to be used to get a quick response. Unfortunately, many ignore E-mails, and some respond if they want to. If they do not respond to them, you know what their response is. Generally, good news comes by telephone and bad news by an E-mail or a letter.

Mistakes, Responsibilities, and Discipline:
3.37 Everyone Makes Mistakes

Successful ones learn from their mistakes, while the losers keep on making the same mistakes and expect different results. Recognizing one's mistake is difficult. It is like finding a scar or a birthmark on the bottom of one's own seat.

If you do find your mistakes, ask yourself why and how you made those mistakes and avoid them. If you have hurt someone inadvertently, admit it and ask for forgiveness. Apology should be genuine. Good leaders admit their mistakes and learn from them. They learn to take criticism seriously but not personally. Others will either blame someone else or berate themselves in private. Accepting your mistakes teaches you to be humble. Elbert Hubbard[26]comments, *"The greatest mistake you can make in life is to be continually fearing you will make one."* The fear of failure stops many in achieving their goals. Two good sayings are, *"The rule for overcoming fear is to head right into it"*, and *"The Fear of the unknown is the hardest one to deal with."* Use probabilities to combat the fear of making a mistake in your actions. The Bible quote, Matthew 55, is, *"Blessed are the meek, for they shall inherit the earth."*

3.38 Discipline

If you cannot control your actions, you have no discipline. More people get into trouble with what they say than what they do. Talk is cheap and some do not foresee any consequences for their actions. Uncontrollable mouths cause more divorces and problems in life. Cheaters are blind. They think they are above all the ethics, rules and regulations. Everyone should expect discipline and accountability from all, including themselves, politicians, bureaucrats, and the ones they deal with in daily life.

3.39 Hubris

Hubris is an exaggerated pride or self-confidence. I was visiting with one of the teachers in my children's grade school, where the school separated the exceptionally bright students from the other students. The teacher of the exceptional student program told the parents to encourage their children to feel superior over other students. This is intellectual arrogance. Smart people are not always wise in common sense.

It is good to have confidence, but intellectual arrogance limits anyone in competing later in life. If they do not succeed at a stage in life, they become failures.

3.40 Always Do Things with Class

If you just do enough to get by, you will be doing that for the rest of your life. If you do more than necessary, you will reap the benefits in the future and you will feel better. Others will respect you too.

3.41 Rumors Hurt

A young man started a false rumor about an old man, a curmudgeon. The rumor spread like a wild-fire. The young man realized that he made a mistake in starting this rumor. He felt bad for his judgment and asked the old man for his forgiveness. In addition, he wanted to know what he could do to pay for the injustice he did towards the old man. The old man thought for a while and asked the young man to take a feather pillow to the top of the mountain, rip the pillow, spread the feathers and come back to see him. The young man did that and came back to the old man. He asked his forgiveness again and asked the old man what else he could further do to pay back for his sin. The old man told the young man to go back to the mountain and collect all the feathers he spread. The young man said that he could not do that, as it is not possible to collect all the feathers he spread. The old man said that the rumors spread like the feathers and retracting them is like collecting all the feathers.

Chapter Four:
Plan for the Future

Basics:
4.1 Basic Human Needs and Passions
We want to do well in life and want everyone to like us. Some needs we cannot live without, such as food, water, air, etc., for survival. Some crave money, control and love; some want to achieve great things; and others do their duty and are useful to the society. We are what we are. We can only play with what we have and how we play dictates our successes and failures.

4.2 Precious Commodities
The precious commodities we have are time, nourishment, clean water, clean air, friends, and children. Without most of these, we cannot survive. Time gets shorter and shorter as we get older and older. Effective use of time becomes a necessity. Money for time is a good trade. For example, buying a tool, such a screw driver, makes more sense than searching for it for a long time. We need to learn to use our mind, money, time, tools etc. to achieve our goals.

Without nourishment, we cannot survive more than a few days. A good dinner makes everyone at ease. May-be that is the reason politicians have elaborate dinners before discussions with their counterparts. Having a nice meal makes one relaxed. May-be that is one of the reasons why young men treat their dates with fancy dinners.

We take water and air for granted. Rainwater is better than tap water for the plants, grass, and for the humans. One can see the difference after a nice quiet rain. Some consider clean air as a tradable commodity and trade for cheap gasoline or cheap power. If we continue to pollute the air we breathe, it will result in illnesses. We take things seriously only when they affect us. We will solve them only when we have no choice. A popular version of Samuel Taylor Coleridge's quote is, *"Water, water everywhere but not a drop to drink."* Without air, we cannot survive. Without clean air, we will be sick. Without, nourishment we will die. Without children, there is no future for humanity.

Without our ancestors, we will not exist. We need friends. Aristotle[27] describes a friend, as *"A friend is a second self."* Unlike a relative, we choose our friends.

4.3 Get a Calendar for Your Activities

It is important to write down meeting schedules, social activities, etc. If you do not, you may arrange to have two appointments at the same time. You go to your dentist to get your teeth cleaned. After the cleaning, you make an appointment for the next cleaning. The date and time is in your subconscious mind. Time passes and a few days before going to the dentist, you need to set a day and time for an important meeting. It seems like the date and time you selected for the dentist is in your subconscious mind, but going to the dentist is not in your mind. So, you pick that day and time for your important meeting. Carrying an appointment book alleviates such problems.

4.4 Plan and Implement

Most of us think that we can start doing anything at any time. This is highly inefficient, as we are planning and implementing it at the same time. This does not allow our thoughts to mature. We do not start driving cross-country without having a map. If we do not know where we are going, we will go someplace, and may not be happy. If we plan the next day's activities, it is easier to get started on the work in the morning. Others may be needed and they need to plan as well. Planning gives a structure and allows our mind to implement and improve it subconsciously.

4.5 Do Not Force Things to Fit in Your Life

An old saying by an unknown author is, *"Life is not a puzzle with pieces that I can force. Rather, it is a tapestry made of colorful threads woven by a hand I cannot see."*

Successful ones plan, focus and pace their activities. They achieve their goals. Unsuccessful ones do things perfunctorily.

4.6 Learn Basic Skills

Be proficient in basics like writing, speaking, and computer skills. The earlier you learn the basics, the better off you are later in life. The ones who acquire basics and people skills will be successful.

Whether you are a preacher, teacher, engineer, doctor, lawyer, or whatever profession you might be in, you have to be a salesperson to succeed. Learn to be a good salesperson. Associate with winners, and avoid trouble-makers and losers.

Good writing and speaking skills are important to have. Once you have mastered these skills, you can use them all your life. Be polite to everyone. If you are, it will help you a long way toward achieving your goals. Individuals with people skills without talents are charlatans. Think before you speak or act. Do not lose control of yourself. If you are in Rome, act like a Roman. If you want to be treated nice, act and do the same.

4.7 Unit Measures

We use unit measures based on percentages, such as a raise to measure one's value to his employer. When we are young and work hard, we get raises, and the raises have a compounding effect. If we do not give our full effort in our work, our raises will be low. We will have a hard time catching up with what we could have if we had worked hard in our early part of our life.

Young ones feel that they have time on their side, and they fritter away this important commodity, time. Whereas when you are old, time left is small.

Grade point average (GPA) is a measure of a student's performance. It is a per unit measure, usually on a four-point scale. It is hard to raise your GPA, but it is easy to let it slide. If you make a low grade, there is no way that you can make a four-point average.

4.8 Fix Before They Break

We are living in a wonderful time in the twenty-first century. We have airplanes and cars to go from one place to another, stoves and microwave ovens to cook food, refrigerators to preserve food, washers to wash clothes, dryers to dry clothes, dish washers to wash dishes, televisions to watch the news, CD players and stereos to listen to music, lawn-mowers to mow lawns, etc. It is normal that things go wrong from time to time. If not maintained properly, they break down at inopportune times. Regular maintenance is the key. It is cheaper to keep things in shape than fix them when they break.

It is even more important with families. Attend to the problems that arise before minor problems become major. Human mind feeds negative thoughts. Watch these signs, and terminate them. Investing in negative emotions is like aiding your worst enemy!

4.9 Accumulation of Money

A river has to have many tributaries before it is a great river. A tree has to have a solid root system forming a base below its trunk before it is a strong tree. Similarly, one needs to have income from several sources to accumulate money. In recent history, people have accumulated massive amounts of money through stocks. Investing in one company may not always produce the growth required to accumulate large amounts. Diversity is necessary to have a steady growth. Athletes, in recent years, have acquired large amounts of money through one source, i.e., playing a sport using their athletic prowess. They become rich in a short time, and they do not give enough thought towards their future. Many of these lose money by not diversifying their efforts in investments.

It is necessary to make money for survival. To flourish, you need to know and act how to use it effectively to achieve your goals. Do not depend on your present organization to support you when you retire. Start on stable investments that allow for growth. Look at averages rather than instantaneous gains or losses. Real estate investment is one of the best ways for steady growth. Population is going to grow, and land is limited. It will appreciate in value. This country's tax system allows for depreciation and improvements on investments. If you are leasing your property, repair and remodel your property as needed. Follow Pres. and Mrs. Lyndon Johnson's[28] advice, *"The best fertilizer for a man's land is the footsteps of its owners."* Retirement is a serious step. Build your portfolio for your family and for your retirement so that you can do the things that make you happy in your life.

Realities in Life:
4.10 Sharing News, Good and Bad

Sharing good news multiplies ones happiness. Sharing sad news divides ones sorrow. Good-hearted ones share. Unhappy ones share only what they want to share.

4.11 Hard Bumps in Life

In relationships, bumps and heartaches are inevitable. Young couples can find their relationship strong or weak by doing things like remodeling their house. For older couples, the tests are building a new house or a marriage in the family. Having a sick child can strain or make the family stronger. Strong bond between couples always helps.

Between friends, conflicts will arise if both are looking for the same job or promotion. Relations between colleagues tend to be formal. Learning the realities becomes an important lesson in anyone's life!

4.12 Dealing with Certain People

Deal with ones who have a what-you-see-is-what-you-get personality. Be careful with ones who have a hidden agenda. They are more interested in their own interests and less interested in you. In any relationship, find out what kind of people you are dealing with. If you find a person tends to be introverted with a hidden agenda, be careful. If you want to be friends with people, make sure they play by the rules of life that everyone agrees. When things are inevitable, accept them and move on.

4.13 See What People Do Rather Than What They Say

Many do not really mean their statements. They use words to make others happy, or show their magnanimity. In any relationship, find what kind of a person he or she is. If he or she is not honest or trustworthy, watch out. This individual will make use of you and will not be there when you need.

4.14 Tolerance, Humility, and Respect for Others

Highly aggressive ones have very little tolerance and less humility. They are brash and tend to live in their own limelight. These may succeed in life but are a burden on others. People can be successful without being rude.

No one can buy trust and respect. They have to be earned. It is better to be respected than liked. Leaders with tolerance and humility have respect from their associates, their supervisors, and the ones they lead. They have control in their actions. In life, they will be successful as individuals.

4.15 Convincing Others

It is almost impossible to convince someone's mind after he makes his decision. Asking someone to change his mind implies that you are questioning his thinking process. Students with a low grade in a class think that they can convince their teacher to give them a better grade. Chances of changing a grade are minimal.

If a group makes a particular decision, they stay with that decision, unless there is strong evidence that they have made a mistake.

4.16 Compartmentalization

In engineering, a system is designed in parts. First, several people can simultaneously design the system. If one of the parts is not working properly, it allows for redesigning that part and replacing it without replacing the whole system.

Home life affects our work, as we are not robots. When things are bad in one part of our life, it hurts. Separate your problems into compartments, i.e., compartmentalize.

4.17 Boring Jobs

Most people spend more time on their work than with their family. Successful people are happy with their jobs. Unsuccessful ones treat their job as work and are unhappy. A job is boring if the work is repetitive and does not require much thinking. Find another job if you are getting bored. Most jobs require thinking. When you apply your brain, every job becomes lively. If your job is not challenging, find creative ways to make your job more enjoyable. As an example, if you are on an assembly line, you may be able to come up with a new simple tool that improves the efficiency of the system. If you look for good aspects in your work, just like in life, you will find them.

Chapter Five:

My Experiences in Education

General Thoughts:
5.1 Education, the Equalizer

Education is the greatest equalizer. An educated child of a peasant can compete with rich children. Because of his background, he has the drive to work hard and show everyone that a child of a peasant can rise to the top in any organization. The new leaders are the innately talented; they are not born rich. Education with common sense will propel anyone to succeed.

5.2 Selection of a University

High school and college students want to know which university they should go to for further studies. There are universities that are poor, average, good, and excellent. It is better to go to a smaller university for an undergraduate degree, where they have a close relationship between students and faculty. At well-known universities, graduate students tend to teach the lower-level classes. For a graduate program, it is better to a go to a prestigious university. Universities are laboratories for new ideas!

5.3 College Students

Some students are not interested in learning the material and are only interested in how to get through a program with a minimal amount of effort. Keeping up with homework allows a student to do better than the one who crams before exams. Cramming does not allow a student to retain important information.

Some students would rather read a newspaper or work on homework for the next class. They feel they are quietly reading or working on a problem and not disturbing anyone. In reality, they are distracting the teacher and the fellow students' attention. Some instructors ignore such, as they do not like confrontation. If a teacher gives better grades than the students deserve, it is time for the teacher to find another vocation.

5.4 Nesting Instincts and College Life

During my stay at Michigan State University in the dorm, playing bridge every weekend used to be a part of our entertainment. Most of the players were young, and many of them were engineering majors. One of the players was a middle-aged man who traveled all over the world. He went through rough times in his life. He was a resident philosopher/adviser for the residents. Many times conversation turned to dating practices. An engineering student used to ask for advice about his problems of not getting dates with some of the pretty girls on campus. He noted that the liberal arts majors do not have such problems. The resident philosopher used to say, *"Wait until you are a senior and you will not have a problem. During the early stages of college life, students are looking for enjoyment. Engineering majors generally do not have as much time to spend compared to liberal arts majors, as they carry bigger loads to graduate and the courses are difficult. When they become seniors, they are attractive to the coeds that are ready to settle. Engineers are industrious and can get jobs with a good pay. Nesting instincts tell the coeds that engineers are good husbands."*

5.5 College Life

College life is one of the nicest times of anyone's life. Each semester has a beginning, and an end. When the semester is over, students can relax. There are breaks, including fall and spring breaks, Christmas holidays, etc. Many of the students have support from their families. Others have to do part-time jobs to support themselves and/or take loans to continue their education.

Students are the only ones who do not complain when they are getting less (education) than what they expected. They enjoy having classes cancelled. The fewer courses they are required to take, the better they feel.

It takes about two years one to specialize in a subject. In engineering, a master's degree gives the engineer an opportunity to work on product development and research, provides a faster track in promotions, and even allows him to be an administrator. When two people come up for a promotion, one with a bachelor's degree and the other with a master's degree, the candidate with a master's degree will invariably get the job. A master's candidate prefers to work for a person with at least a master's degree.

If one wants to teach at a university, work at a research lab, or work at one of the national labs, doctorate degree is almost a necessity. A doctoral student goes through several hoops, including preliminary exams, qualifying exams, and a final oral exam on the dissertation. The ones that survive the preliminary exams continue taking classes and select a topic to do research. The student finds out that research is like picking fruit from a tree and it gets harder and harder as the early researchers have picked the low-hanging fruit. Initially, he hopes that his research will be of the caliber of receiving a Nobel Prize. As time passes, the student is going to have difficulties and hopes that he will be proud of his work. In the later stages, he hopes that he will be satisfied with his thesis if his committee approves it. Even failures in research and in life, are important to note, as they indicate the paths to avoid. Interestingly, good scientists are not born. They are created.

5.6 Union Cards

To be a professor at a major university in this country, it is necessary to have a PhD. There are many with masters or even a B.S. degree with experience that are more knowledgeable than some of the PhDs. Research laboratories like to have their employees to have doctoral degrees. In that sense, a PhD degree is a union card.

5.7 Universities Use a Caste System in Hiring Their Faculty

People criticize the caste system in India, but there is a subtle form of this everywhere in the world. Universities like to hire faculty from universities that have a higher or equal rank than their own. To see this, look at a university catalogue of your choice and see where their faculty came from. The catalogues provide the list of their faculty, their publication record, their terminal degrees, and the universities they graduated from. If a graduate student is interested in a faculty position, he should get a degree from a prestigious university in his area of interest.

5.8 Scientists

A budding scientist learns basics of research, discovers the beauty of research with new ideas. He needs to be a self-starter. Passion and persistence are needed to be successful. A relaxed mind is a creative mind. Sir James Dewar[29] said, "*Minds are like parachutes. They only function when they are open.*" Hockey star, Wayne Gretzky[30] used to say, "*Skate where the puck is going, not where it's been,*" a good way to think about a research topic. True scientists are skeptical. They believe in an idea if it can be proven.

There are two common types of scientists. After basic training in research, they continue doing research. Others just love to do research, as they get pleasure in finding the unknown. The first type of researcher follows the rules and is a model researcher for the administrators. His research is derivative. The second type of researcher has unique ideas. He knows how to conceptualize, plan, and execute his research. He is a pioneer in his field. He has very little tolerance for others that are not as proficient as he is in his field and is on his own stratosphere. A successful scientist needs innate intuition and talent, and, more importantly the tenacity to succeed in his research.

5.9 Writers and Scientists Have a Lot in Common

Engineers design systems that work like a fine-tuned machine. Scientific and mathematical proofs have to follow logic. Novelists have to be logical in developing their story and, at the same time keep the interest of the reader. In a similar way, to be successful in life, one has to follow with sound reasoning.

Teaching:
5.10 Teachers

To teach discipline, you need to have discipline. To teach research, you must have done research. A saying is, "*The ones who cannot do research teach.*" This is not always true. However, an outstanding researcher-teacher is rare.

There are several kinds of teachers. Some stand in front of a classroom and just talk; some explains the material; and the best teachers demonstrate. When students come for help, they do not give the answers. Instead, they ask questions and extract the answers. If a teacher gives the answers without explanation, students do not learn. It is like giving fish from your icebox instead of teaching how to fish in a lake.

Good teachers take criticism from their students with dignity. Poor teachers cannot handle criticism. They become defensive.

5.11 A Good Professor
Students dislike a faculty member who gives open-ended problems and exams. They dislike it even more if the problems have more than one solution, such as design problems. The problems in industry and in real life do not have a single solution, but a number of solutions. Picking a solution that fits the best in a situation requires several levels of thinking. The design-oriented instructors train the students to tackle real-life problems. They teach them how to learn and do not spoon-feed the material. The rewards for the teachers come much later when they hear successes of their students.

A good professor is a good listener and a good human being. He asks the right questions to make the student think for himself.

5.12 Graduate Faculty and Recruiting
One of the objectives of a research professor is building a research program for his graduate students, who need support. Without good research, faculty cannot attract funding. In turn, they cannot attract good graduate students to do the research. It is like the proverbial phrase, *chicken or the egg that comes first.*

The best researchers may not be the best recruiters and vice versa. Successful researchers have to be good teachers. No one can teach the innate talents to anyone. Professors can only teach the mechanics, provide ideas, and ask probing questions that help the students discover their innate talents to find the solutions to problems.

5.13 Raising Funds at Universities
Faculty successes depend upon their innovative publications and fund-raising abilities. The successful ones get good raises, fast promotions, and kudos at a university. Funding agencies look at the need for the proposed research, publication record of the applicant, and the potential for student support. It is easier and better to raise funds, say $10k, from ten organizations than raising $100k from one organization.

It helps if the applicant is a well-known researcher or he is from a well-known university. Younger faculty members have a harder time attracting funds. Associating with senior faculty members, doing joint research, and writing research proposals is a good way for them. Showing support to students show that the proposed funding helps the donor organization. A successful professor is a good fund-raiser, a good teacher, a good researcher, a mentor, and a good citizen at a university.

5.14 Types of Arrogance

Intellectual arrogance is prevalent at universities, at scientific laboratories, at high places in government, etc. Some look down on the ones who are not as proficient in their specialty or talent as they are, exhibiting their intellectual arrogance. They are loners and associate with selected ones. Financial arrogance goes with rich people who dominate others with their money. This has been in existence over the history of humankind.

White-collar employees feel superior to the blue-collar ones, as they do not have to do any work with their hands. They feel insulted to do hands-on work showing their white-collar arrogance. Blue-collar workers do not have the same respect in our society as the white-collar workers. Blue-collar workers are not hesitant to say that white-collar workers are awkward and clumsy, i.e., *all thumbs*, and cannot do any work with their hands showing their blue-collar arrogance. Many of the situation-comedy TV programs show the ineptness of both the white- and blue-collar workers.

Religious zealots feel their religion is better than anyone else's religion. They are ruthless and are willing to sacrifice their own lives or take the life of people from other sects, or other religions, exhibiting their religious arrogance. The ones with race arrogance think their race is better than other races. They put down anyone from other races to avoid competing with them. The elected officials think they are the decision makers and not the servants of the electorate showing their political arrogance. Some of the males and females feel superior to their counterparts, thus exhibiting sex arrogance. Arrogant people tend to be blunt in dealing with others. They are capable of hurting their prey using their sharp tongue like a knife cutting butter.

Performance and Ethics:
5.15 Examinations and Testing

Average measurements give better measures than instantaneous measurements. Being a teacher for over forty years, I used to give four different exams during each semester, one easy, one hard, one long, and one a standard exam. The reason for these is that some students do well with a hard exam, some do well with a long exam, and others do well with an easy exam. However, the final grade is always based on a curve, i.e., the scores are added together at the end of the semester and grades are plotted. The grade A is for the top students until there is a breakpoint and this process is continued for grades B, C, etc. The ones who have received B's have a higher grade than C's and there is a break in the curve between B's and C's. The reason for a standard exam is to compare the students with the present and the previous semesters. It is hard to grade a hard exam, as giving partial credit is difficult. Good ones do well in a hard exam.

Students like their teachers to drop a score of an exam, such as a bad grade in one of the exams. Omitting the outliers in data analysis from the data is standard. In my view, it is not fair to students who do average work on every test. Interestingly, it is easier to measure failures compared to successes in education. It is true in life as well.

5.16 Engineering Students Have a Good Work Ethic

Many engineers come from farm families. Many of the universities in this country are A&M Colleges, where A is for agriculture and M is for Mechanic Arts. Most farmers send their children to A&M colleges. Farmers have a good work ethic; their life is harsh, as they are at nature's mercy and their income is cyclical depending upon the weather. Farms get smaller and smaller as the properties divide from generation to generation. The kids from small farms have to work hard to survive. They are not afraid to work with their hands, unlike city kids. They are highly focused on their work. When they come to college, they work hard and do well.

One of the bankers in our town told me the following. "*I would hire an engineer any day, even though he or she may not have any business education background. Engineers go through a rigorous education program and it takes more than four years to go through in engineering to graduate. They have an analytical mind with common sense and are goal-oriented. They know their limitations. When they cannot figure out something, they ask for help. They know hard work, know how important a bank is for families, and know how to help them to succeed. When they become leaders, they will take care of their employees and will do well in life. We like those type of individuals.*"

5.17 Engineers and Contingencies

Engineers consider, plan, and execute long-range activities for possible events with contingencies. They are trained in basics and can adapt to future contingencies. They are purpose-driven. In an engineering design problem, there is more than one solution. Engineers select the best solution, based upon the specifications including the reliability, cost effectiveness, and simplicity for the system design. They are cognizant of production cost-benefit ratio of their product and produce products that are better and cheaper. For example, the prices of electronic products, such as computers, televisions, radios, etc., are significantly lower than when they were introduced and they are getting cheaper and cheaper every year and, at the same time, the quality of them is getting better. Today's society is a throwaway society. If things go wrong with a gadget, we throw it away and buy a new one, as it is more cost-effective. Remember one of Warren Buffett's[31] quotes and is, *"Price is what you pay. Value is what you get."* In the new era, we have planned obsolescence. Engineers are trained to be adaptable to the survival and betterment of the society!

5.18 Performance of Male and Female Students in Engineering

Most engineering classes have mostly male students. The quality of performance of them is usually good with a few exceptions. Female engineering students know that engineering is a difficult field and want to be part of that profession. Some of them get into engineering because their fathers are engineers. On the average, female engineering students do extremely well and later as engineers. Woman's perspectives should be considered in product designs. They are highly recruited by industry, government, and universities with higher pay than men.

5.19 Measures on Men and Women

Historically men had to find food by hunting and spent most of the time outside home. They enjoyed the physical strength and the intimidation it allows. Women stayed home taking care of the home and the children. They had to become multi-taskers. They are more tenacious, complicated, patient and smarter to compensate for lesser physical strength than men. They had time to analyze human nature and learned to be smarter in the world of common sense. Men use their objective prowess in evaluating an individual or situation.

Women use their subjective prowess in evaluating an individual or situation. They are better evaluators in judging people than men.

5.20 Why the Immigrants Do Better Than the Natives Do

Three types of immigrants come to this country for education. The first type of immigrants come from well-to-do families and can finance their education; the second type are children of highly educated parents; and the third type are ones with little resources but are highly motivated to have more than what they had in their native land. They have the drive to succeed and the fear that things may not work out for them in the new land. When they come to this country, they come with a suitcase, a small amount of cash, and an undergraduate education. They do not have a safety net in case they fail. They know they have an equal footing as the other international students. They constantly strive to get better. They feel the natives have an edge in getting a better position than they can. They have to show a superior performance to get the same accolades. This drives the immigrants to do well in their new land. They tend to be meek socially but aggressive in achieving their goals, as they have high pressure of expectations from their families. They tend to do extremely well in school. They are more interested in hard sciences and many of them prefer medical schools.

Performance of children of immigrants tends to be better than the performance of children of natives. Children of immigrant's intensity in education tend to be less than their immigrant parents' intensity.

For the Future:
5.21 Interviewing for a Job

I was visiting with two students who are planning to interview with the same company. I gave the same information to both about the company. One read the details ahead of time. The information he did not know, he looked it up. He prepared his own documents before he went for an interview. The other one decided to wait to study the documents the night before the interview. He realized that he could not understand the material anyway and did not have enough time to find more information. The first one got the job, whereas the second one did not.

For a job interview, study the company's products, find what they are looking for in their employees, and provide information how you can contribute to the growth of that company. Stress your strong points in your résumé. Make sure that you can fit and succeed in that company's environment.

5.22 Networking
A successful person uses his abilities and gets help from family, friends, and colleagues. Contacts are important to find employment. Professional society meetings are ideal for good contacts, as there are meetings, parties, etc. Nature provided us with two hands, one hand to carry a drink and the other hand to shake. That is our culture today in hunting for a job. Make use of all the contacts.

5.23 References
When universities or companies look for individuals as students or employees, they rely on the candidate's references. As a first step, they request the names of people that know the candidate well. Most of the references usually give good reviews on the candidate. As anyone can infer if the candidate thinks that a particular reference may give a bad review, he will not provide that individual as a reference. The one who is hiring values the references that are in the same organization as the candidate.

One of the old adages is that mountains look smooth from far away, whereas they are rough nearby. That is, the closer you are, the better you can see the details. Many times a recruiter can get candid references from individuals that he himself knows personally. In these days of lawsuits, however, one has to be careful about using references not listed by the candidate. A detailed reference letter is always respected by the recruiters. An overall picture of the individual is just as important as the details of the individual's professional background.

5.24 Deselecting Phrases in Job Interviews
Any time you are in a job interview, the interviewer is looking to find out how you react in situations. In the interview, let the interviewer take the lead. He can hire only a few. He is looking for a person who will do well and be a good representative for his company. Companies have a campus interview and a plant interview. For the informal campus interview, the interviewer may not even be in your field. He can only ask some general questions of how you would react. He is trying to select a few good candidates, as his job is to separate "*the wheat from chaff.*" In the plant interview, there may be technical questions. The plant interviewer looks for delimiting phrases. As an example, in

today's world, the computer plays a major role. He may ask, *"Do you like to work on computers?"* If you say, *"I hate computers,"* you are out from further consideration. What do you think of working late hours and traveling? In a company organization, you have to be flexible; consequently, traveling is another sticky point with companies. Depending upon the type of position you are applying for, you may have to travel a lot or make an occasional trip or two. If you say, *"I do not like to travel,"* that is a delimiter. If you say, *"I do not like to travel, but I need to plan ahead because of my family,"* they will understand that. If they need someone who needs to travel on a moment's notice, they will not hire you. They will recognize your forthrightness and find a position that you can fit in their organization. *"I like to work by myself"* is a delimiting statement for any organization, as the goal for it is to have the workforce to work in unison.

Companies are there to provide products and/or services to make a profit. It needs honest individuals who can make money for them. They are interested in ones that are capable, flexible and stable to fit in their organization.

5.25 Read Fiction and Nonfiction

Fiction presents what may be plausible. Fiction writers have imagination and give freedom to their minds to come up with stories. A good writer or a researcher produces consistent material. The result is a controlled imagination. Understand the difference between fiction and reality of life.

Victors write history. Losers are only observers. You cannot always trust the accuracy of history unless and until the losers have a chance to contribute towards it. Do not believe the printed material to be accurate. Always check before accepting it to be accurate. You can learn how others triumphed from their problems by reading their biographies. A. G. Grayling[32] states, *"Good biography requires the psychologist's eye, the historian's nose, and the novelist's feel for narrative."*

Engineers tend to concentrate on technical literature and become one-dimensional individuals. They should broaden their minds by reading fiction and associating with people with different backgrounds.

5.26 Proposals, Documents, and Presentations

Before submitting a proposal or a document, make sure that the document is the best to your satisfaction. One of the hardest problems is stating the problem itself. The plans must be worthy of consideration by others. Journal reviewers and funding agencies like to find problems with the proposals and documents before they decide on them. It is easy to put a negative mark on a document if there are errors, even simple ones.

Engineers have to make presentations from time to time. They tend to present raw facts, which go over the head of most of the listeners. A better way is to present the results in the form of a story. In the initial presentation, the speaker should identify why he did what he did. What are the main results? Why are they important? Minimize the mundane mathematical details. If there is a new technique, it should be included. Avoid platitudes. Present only important details. At the end of the presentation, it is important to point out the results and compare with some of the earlier works. Give the interested audience enough time to ask questions and get them interested in your work.

5.27 University Search Committees

One of the activities of a faculty member is to serve on a committee in a search process for a faculty member, department head, dean, or some other position at the university. The committee is supposed to give a list of three or four names to the upper administrator giving the option to select one from the list that fits his (or her) interest. Some of the upper administrators think they know better than the faculty and want to have their own imprint on the search process. There is always a possibility that the administrator may leave after he selects, whereas most of the faculty will be staying. There is a tug of war that goes on between the faculty and the upper administrator. Interestingly, in selecting a Pope, the College of Cardinals meets in secrecy and will not announce their selection until they have selected a pope who has 100 percent support. That might be a way of choosing a candidate for an administrative position in a university.

Chapter Six:
Professional Life

Life Changes:
6.1 Changes in Professional Life

At some time in life, you may face the prospect of changing your job or even retiring. What is the best time? Move on if you do not face challenges in your work. Quit if your peers do not respect you. Do not want to leave too soon, but never too late, either. An old saying is, *"Don't run from something. Run to something you desire."* Some wait too long before they admit that they are incapable of giving the effort of their pay.

Many employees leave when they are flying high, even though the company needs them. They find a new place of employment, rev things up, and continue this process until they cannot go any further. This takes a toll on anyone and his family.

6.2 Change of Plans

If you have been working on a project and it is not going well, do not change it precipitously. You do not repair an airplane in flight or change horses in the middle of a stream. Analyze your original plan, sleep on it, and correct your plans gradually.

6.3 Everyone Is Replaceable

Before you think highly of yourself, remember that you are replaceable. Nobody is invincible. A friend, a successful administrator, used to say, *"When I feel that I am important, I keep reminding myself that my efforts are like churning water in a bucket resulting in ripples for a short time. After they are gone, the effect is reduced to zero."* We are like bubbles in the ocean. Do not think of yourself that you are God-given to humanity or a demigod. You have talents as well as faults. Everyone contributes to the society. Always have your feet on a solid ground and give more than you take.

6.4 Goals of an Employee
Everyone in an organization should have a plan to make the organization better. Each one should focus on their mission and not worry about others' actions, as long as they are following a path of a desirable endeavor and not hurting someone on purpose.

6.5 An Ideal Employee
An ideal employee does not mind who gets the credit, as long as the job at hand is completed properly. He is the unsung hero of the organization. It is the duty of the leader to identify and reward him. Selfish employees want recognition for everything they do and look after themselves more than their organization. They tend to be backstabbers.

6.6 Enthusiasm and Salesmanship
You have to be enthusiastic to be successful in whatever you are doing. You have to be a salesman with tenacity to succeed.

Leaders:
6.7 A Leader
A leader is not born; he is made. He makes mistakes. When he recognizes it, he admits it, and takes action to correct them. He is a good listener with a pleasant personality. He is proactive rather than reactive to the causes he believes in, takes a stand on issues regardless of personal consequences and takes ownership for his actions.

6.8 Leaders of an Organization
A leader has many problems. If he is close to one of his assistants, then the others dislike that relationship. There is always a possibility that the supervisor may have to make a decision on this individual. Any decision he makes on this

individual makes it very painful, especially if he goes against that individual. If he makes a favorable decision, then the others will feel that it is a biased decision. It is good to get advice from a levelheaded senior individual in the organization. Decisions have consequences. The leader needs to be nice to the person that is under scrutiny. No one loses by being nice. The employee appreciates this quality. In the future, if the leader needs help from the employee, he will be helpful. The quality of an individual comes out when he faces uncertainty and opposition. When things are going well, any idiot can run the organization. When things are not going well, it needs a real leader. Dr. Martin Luther King, Jr.[33], a Nobel Laureate, stated, *"A genuine leader is not a searcher for consensus but a molder of consensus."* Leader's greatest resource is people. His task is providing a proper framework for his people to succeed.

A leader cannot fight on all fronts. If one goes duck hunting, he cannot shoot several ducks at one time. He has to concentrate on one duck and shoot one at a time. A supervisor is one individual managing several employees. He may make some happy and others unhappy. The unhappy folks do not forget. They will get together; and if there are enough people to oppose a supervisor, they will try to undermine him.

A leader needs to take bold steps. He should not confuse leadership with popularity. Some assistants may be unhappy and oppose the leader at every step in his actions. Others may not like his decisions and may not agree with him but respect his decisions. A leader should be kind to these and find out why some disagree with his plans. Some may agree with the leader's decisions and support him in his decisions because they may be afraid of him. Leaders should consider such possibility.

A leader should be a caring one. He may get upset and even lash out at some that complain. That is a no-no. An effective way to deal with this anger is write down the frustrations on a piece of paper, put it in the desk, and look at it after a few days. If it turns out that it is not necessary to lash out, tear up the note. Visiting with the individual in a calm manner and resolving the conflict is the best. A leader should have friends outside his organization. With outside friends, he can have frank discussions.

6.9 Selection of a Leader

Leadership is changing for the better. A leader is disciplined with good temperament, integrity and communications skills. He has good strategic skills and empathy for others. He attracts individuals to his organization that are smarter than him and are loyal. He knows that he cannot buy loyalty, from anyone, especially from his employees. He respects them when they point out the mistakes he is making. He helps his employees achieve their goals and grow. He is a good mentor. He knows that ego should never come between him and his job. If the organization he is in-charge-of fails, he is accountable. He understands the German proverb, *"The higher a monkey climbs, the more he shows his behind."* A good leader does not have the following characteristics:

He is self-centered and acts like a showman; is arrogant and feckless; and attacks anyone that criticizes him. Gets easily rattled and does not keep his promises. He finds a scapegoat to blame for his failures. He brags what he can do for his organization. Sells his soul to get what he wants. He would stab others, including his friends, to help himself.

Does not respect the views of others, especially his assistants. When he disagrees with his supervisors, he bad-mouths them in private and lauds them in public.

He has to have control of everything in his life. As a result, no one can grow under his leadership, just like nothing grows under an East Indian banyan tree.

6.10 Supervisor and the Weakest Link

A supervisor needs to be cognizant of the weakest links in his organization and take action. If he does not, he will see troubles down the road. He needs to make sure that assignments are completed and satisfactory in time. What should a supervisor do with unreliable people that do not pull their weight? There are two options: Get rid of them; or, put them in positions that will not jeopardize the mission of the organization. The supervisor needs to keep a detailed file on the performance of the unreliable employees.

6.11 Leaders Should Get Advice from All Sides

An effective leader consults his employees from all sides, especially if he is trying to make a decision. If he is leaning towards one side, it is doubly important that the leader visit with individuals with opposite views. Note the advice by John C. Collins[34] that, *"Always mistrust a subordinate who never finds fault with his superior!"*

Historically, successful kings used to go incognito to find out what was happening in their country, especially when things were not going well. With present-day communications, we have pundits on TV, or talking heads, giving opinions from all sides. It is important to separate the signal from noise, i.e., separate wheat from the chaff. The value of free advice is often equal to what it costs.

6.12 Captain and the Sergeant

People control through others, like a captain controls his troops through a sergeant. For the troops, a sergeant is bad, but the captain is nice. A sergeant uses powerful words to make members of his troop behave properly. If it does not work, then he uses the weapon that he will report to the captain. Similarly, supervisors, in general, say that they are following the orders from upper management to get their ways.

6.13 Leader's Statements

A leader of an organization should watch what he says, as everyone gives weight to a leader's statements. A true leader can bring harmony among rival factions. If a leader cannot deliver what he says, his credibility is gone. When he makes a mistake, the entire organization suffers. Some leaders do not admit their mistakes until someone catches them red-handed. He loses respect from his constituency.

6.14 People in Power

When people in power go down, by choice or are forced out, the number of so-called friends goes down and the number of enemies increases. True friends do not change their behavior towards their friends. If the leader did something wrong, his true friends will give counsel and help in overcoming the situation.

6.15 Administrators and Mavericks

Good administrators look at situations in all possible dimensions and come up with a proper solution to a problem. They are good on their feet. They can handle themselves well when they are out of their comfort zone. They can build the right teams with members that can collaborate. Mavericks are highly talented and are idea chasers. They are independent and do not take orders. They follow their own logic and do not like to follow society's standards or norms. They are not money chasers.

Good administrators use mavericks to find the pitfalls in their system and correct its problems. Mavericks have to be careful in their actions, as they are fallible. The smart ones, who are not mavericks, wait for the mavericks to make mistakes. When they do, they pounce on the mavericks, destroying their credibility. Mavericks' lives are difficult and they tend to have many enemies. They need their administrators look after them.

6.16 Idealism and Realism

Good leaders are idealistic with a touch of realism. When dealing with humans, we have to compromise and learn from our failings. It comes with practice and age. Use simple solutions to solve problems. The more complicated the solutions are, the more chances are there to fail.

In any organization, it is inevitable to have a prima donna. He may be successful in a way but destructive to the success of the organization. Success of an organization does not depend upon one individual; it depends on the entire team.

Experience, Organizations, Professions, and Employees:
6.17 Benefits of Experience

Experience gives the knowledge to learn from past mistakes. Young people do not like to learn from older ones. Their arguments are, "*Let us make our own mistakes and we will learn from them.*" This may be true, but learning from the experienced ones shortens the learning process. We go to school and learn from our teachers. We may still make mistakes, but they will be fewer. Enjoy the fruits of the previous generations by taking their advice and learning from their mistakes. Make the system better for the next generation. One of the Chinese sayings is, "*If you want to know the road ahead, ask someone who has traveled it.*" In life, there will always be setbacks. Consulting with experts will help to reduce the number of setbacks. Note that good judgment of one can trump the experience of another.

6.18 Squeaky Wheel Always Gets the Grease

In every society, there are always habitual complainers. They receive more attention than the quiet ones. If you have a squeaky wheel on your bike, you will oil it. If you receive a poor service from an organization, do not hesitate to complain to the managers. Good managers appreciate this as they like to correct the problems.

6.19 White-Collar and Blue-Collar Workers

The mental interaction between a blue-collar and a white-collar worker is interesting. Each side looks down on the other side. If each side respects the other and can admit each side's own weaknesses, the interaction can be pleasant. Those who are talented should do the work. Those who are not should let the talented ones do the appropriate work.

The unfortunate problem is that we do not want to admit to ourselves that we cannot be good in everything we need to do. Admit your limitations. Let the professionals handle the things we are incapable of doing.

Interesting Notes:
6.20 Independent Professions

Of all the professions, working for yourself gives you the most independence. Farming is a good example. Teaching is another one. Academia is very flexible. Making money for others is not worth the effort on your psyche as you are at someone else's mercy. If you want to start your own business, get training in that business. Working in a company in the early stages of your career makes you learn the intricacies of starting your own business. Learn from a good manager how to work with people.

6.21 Organizations for Product Development

One person can make a difference whether in a small or a large organization if he can innovate. Small companies can have quick changes. They can follow the trends of development, whereas a large company has a large moment of inertia and cannot have fast changes. Large companies can set up pools of people to work on several research projects at one time and come up with several new products. The small companies can fold quickly, whereas large companies have more time to change and innovate.

No one can come up with revolutionary ideas on products out of the blue. It requires product knowledge and history. It is best to learn basics in a large company first. Then, if you are innovative, go with a small company. Even start one.

6.22 Everything in Life is a Collection of Modules

We design systems in modules and do the same in life. We check our accounts every month. If they do not balance, we only have to check one month at a time, as balancing the accounts for a year at a time is difficult. We divide time into years, months, weeks, days, minutes, seconds, etc. We have many countries. Each country has states, districts or counties, etc. In college, we have separate classes for English, history, mathematics, etc. We write a book in terms of different chapters with chapters tied together. Life is a drama with actors and scenes. In the same way, we compartmentalize our life's activities in modules to achieve our goals. This makes life simple.

6.23 Stature and Gender

I was talking to a colleague about two capable candidates for an administrative position. I was curious about how our faculty would evaluate these two candidates. I was under the impression that the faculty would look at the candidate's credentials. My colleague said that both have similar records and the taller candidate would be better as an administrator. Shorter people think taller people are better as administrators. Once hired, the advantage evaporates. If you look at the statistics on presidential elections in this country, taller candidates have won more times than the shorter ones. Unfortunately, most look at obese people and say that they may not live long enough time to occupy for a high-pressured administrative positions and not even be considered for the position.

On the average, men tend to be taller than women are. Taller men have more of an advantage compared to shorter men when it comes to marriages, as they have a larger pool of women to marry. Shorter women have more of an advantage compared to taller women when it comes to marriages, as they have a larger pool of men to marry.

Unfortunately, many biases exist in every part of life in this country. For example, in some fields, a woman's pay is lower than a man's is, even though both may have the same credentials. No woman has ever become the President of USA so far. Accomplishments and talents should be the basis in evaluating individuals for any position.

6.24 If You Can Solve a Problem by Paying Money, Pay

Some problems, such as cancer, may not have any solutions; others with solutions cannot be solved because of someone does not cooperate. If you have a solvable problem by spending money, do it, i.e., if you can afford it and not violating any of your tenets.

Service and church organizations have recognized that their members' emotional energy towards their organizations is important. They would like to have their members' time and effort in addition to their money. They will say, "*Do not mistake us. We like to have your money, but your service, efforts, and time are more valuable to the cause.*" If the organizations can convince someone to be of service, he will give money too!

6.25 Organizations
A bird cannot fly if its two wings do not flap at the same time. A marriage cannot succeed if the wife and husband pull in different directions. A two-wheel cart cannot go anywhere if the wheels pull in different directions. When the members of the organization want to go in different directions, the organization may have incidental success, but the overall success will be minimal. A successful organization operates in unison like a well-oiled machine.

In the old days, when companies were trying to hire a leader, they first evaluated the credentials of the individual and checked with his references. Usually, the references included not only his superiors but also his subordinates, especially his secretary. In my view, the candidate's secretary can evaluate his character better than his colleagues can. Throughout history, women, in general, tend to be better judges in evaluating individuals than men are. In the final stages, the selection committee wants to know how the candidate and his wife work as a team. They are looking for a good leader. Can he manage his own family? They are extrapolating the results by observing the couple. If he cannot select a suitable mate, he may not be able to hire a good team and manage.

6.26 Glass Ceilings
In the last century, to be in a leadership position, you had to be a white Anglo-Saxon Protestant. Later on you had to be a white man to be a leader. Since then women, blacks, and other minorities have succeeded in breaking the artificial barriers, referred to as glass ceilings. In 2008, U.S. elected a black President, Pres. Barak Obama, and a breakthrough in societal thinking. Glass ceilings exist in different forms in every society.

Some may take positions with companies to get experience that is not in their field. To be in a leadership role in a particular industry, you have to be trained in the main field of the company. For example, one has to be a geophysicist or a petroleum geologist to be a leader in the petroleum industry.

Engineers cannot reach the higher management level. An advice to a new graduate is to take a job in a good company and get experience. Then change to a company that is in his/her field.

6.27 Feedback in Any Endeavor
Whatever your position is, it helps you to have feedback from clientele. If you did a good job, a nice comment from your client will give a boost to your morale and you may do even better next time. If you did a poor job, you need to know what you did wrong. Constructive comments will help you to improve your performance. Without feedback, finding out what you are doing wrong is difficult. Consulting a senior employee for advice is always helpful. He may have gone through many problems you are going through now. In life, feedback is a basic staple that every human uses!

6.28 Riding a Tiger
You are doing well in your professional life. You would like to relax and slow down. You are afraid to slow down because you may lose the edge you are having. This is like riding a tiger. You are afraid of getting off the tiger, because if you do, the tiger might eat you. It is like hanging onto a cliff and if you relax, you are going to fall. Try to avoid such thoughts. Have a solid plan for your professional activities including how and when to take time off, and stick to that plan.

6.29 The Tortoise and the Hare, an Aesop Fable
In simple words, a hare and a tortoise had a race. The hare bragged about its speed and insulted the tortoise for its slowness. At the start, the hare ran fast and waited for the turtle to come in sight. Thinking that it could run faster than the tortoise, the hare fell asleep. The tortoise moved slowly and won the race. A steady worker is better than a bragging fast-starter!

6.30 Negative Dominates
A bad review on an article or reference dominates a positive one. Every culture has good and bad points. In any selection process, if the members of a committee differ, the negative comments have more of an effect than the positive comments.

When a person talks, most take it literally. Say what you mean. Do not expect others to take it in a positive way. It is better to temper the negative statements about any one, as they are hurtful.

Western culture values hard work, building good economics, and personal freedom. Like any society, bad influences spread fast. When young people from a third world country first embrace bad aspects of Western culture, such as drugs, alcohol, carousing, etc., they ignore the good things in the Western culture.

6.31 Perfectionism

We all like to achieve goals. Some want to have perfection in everything they do, an impossible task. One can try to reach this goal but may never reach it. It gets harder and harder to reach the pinnacle. It is not possible for a student to get 100 percent on his test scores in every class he takes.

We cannot make components with exact values. Electrical engineers use component tolerances as measures in evaluating a circuit. When the required tolerance levels get smaller, the designs get more difficult and therefore more expensive. It is impossible to design and construct a system that is 100 percent perfect in every way. The same is true in life for everyone.

A perfectionist expects every person, action, and result to be ideal even though he is not perfect. Perfectionists tend to be unhappy and are not good leaders.

6.32 Good Starters and Lousy Finishers

If you are looking to hire someone to work for you, find a person who is a good finisher. It does not mean much if you are a good starter unless you can finish what you started. Good finishers are hard to find, as they are rare.

If you are an employer, find someone that strives to complete his job and not someone who gives up easily. Losers give up easily when things are not going their way.

Success or failure in life depends on what a person does in his or her adult life. Successful ones have a good background in school and have a good family support.

Good finishers do not choke. They always stand out!

Chapter Seven:
Lessons from Sports

7.1 Sports

In sports, there are champions, winners and losers. Winners do not cheat! Before one becomes a champion, he has to learn to be a winner. Winners are talented and focused. An injured super athlete thinks about his past successes and asks how and why he was injured. He needs a super coach to bring him back to his old self. Individual sports teach pacing, sportsmanship, and drive. If you are a long-distance runner, you do not run at high speed at the beginning and run out of steam after the first lap. Life is a marathon, not a sprint. It can be perilous. Learn to pace yourself to achieve your goals.

Team sports teach cooperation and good sportsmanship. Unlike politics and religion, discussion on sports is good in group conversations. Success in the sports arena brings in physical arrogance. Some of the athletes ignore their bounds; they do some things beyond the societal norms and get into trouble.

7.2 Individual and Team Sports

The ones who play individual sports, such as running, wrestling, tennis, golf, etc., tend to be high achievers. They know that if they lose, it is their own fault. They are playing against themselves and want to improve. Tennis and golf are sports that are good at any age. Students who play individual sports tend to do much better in school and in life than the students who play team sports. Engineering jobs emulate team sports.

Individual sport teaches young ones to be self-reliant. It helps them grow as individuals. In a team sport, an average player tends to be less aggressive. If things go wrong for a team member, he can blame other team members. Learning to keep composure in adversity is difficult. A good sportsman keeps his composure.

7.3 Winning Brings Unity and Success

If the team is winning, it brings the entire team closer. If the team is losing, there will be finger pointing and blaming others. Good teams win close games.

In sports, we want to win; and in life, we must win. When faced with obstacles that seem insurmountable, we must have the attitude that we have no choice but to win. If we give up, we will certainly not win. If we keep fighting, we have a chance to win. A star athlete's mantra is, *"I am in the flow and cannot lose."*

7.4 Simple Plans are better in Sports, in Systems, and in Life

It is better to have a simple robust game plan. Possibility for breakdowns in complicated plans is greater than in a simpler one in team sports.

High performance systems require expensive and constant maintenance. The designs of such systems require sophisticated methodology. As a rule, the simpler the system is, the easier to maintain. One of the quotes attributed to Leonardo da Vinci[35] is, *"Simplicity is the ultimate sophistication."* Make your life simple!

7.5 Sportsmen and Scientists

The shelf life of an athlete is short. If an athlete does not accept that his/her time has passed and continue to play, he or she will be humiliated. A good athlete can follow many paths after playing his sports, such as becoming part of a coaching staff or a commentator. Everyone has to face reality in life! Scientists have a longer life than athletes do. Both are highly respected in their own domains. Scientists can become managers, professors, or book writers. Good researchers and good fishermen have a lot in common. Good researchers know good research areas to pursue; good fishermen know best fishing locations. Fishermen know how to relax. Researchers cannot stop innovation!

A champion in sports or a good scientist believes in his abilities, trusts his hunches, prepares for his activities, and fights to succeed. He knows when to quit.

7.6 Different Sports

In baseball, the star of the team is the pitcher. His goal is to minimize the opposing teams' offense. Baseball, a game without a clock, is a slow-tempo game. In football, the star of the team is the quarterback. His goal is to move the ball and score touchdowns. The offensive side of the game is incentive based. If they move the ball at least ten yards, they get four more chances to move towards the opponent's goal post. It has controlled violence resulting in injuries. Basketball is fast-paced and is supposed to be a non-contact sport. Bigger and taller players with quickness do well in this sport. When the players do what is best for their team rather their own glory, the team becomes a great team. Offensive players invariably get more accolades than defensive players.

Golf is a cerebral sport. A winner in golf has control of his emotions. It allows for friends and executives to chat and make deals. It requires slow-paced walking with stops. Tennis, a game without a clock, is an expensive sport. Winners do not dwell over lost opportunities. They concentrate on the present and play one point at a time. If one gives the champion a chance, he will generate enough strength to beat his opponent.

Soccer is a cheap and a fast sport. It has all the physical activity with fewer injuries than most other sports. Field hockey is a good sport and is not violent. Ice hockey is a fast game. If you like controlled violence, it is a good sport to watch. Boxing is liked by a very few fans, and disliked by many as the purpose of this sport is knocking the opponent out. If you learn to ride a bike or learn to swim, you can never forget doing them. They are good exercises.

General George S. Patton, Jr.[36] suggestions are useful in war, sports, and in life. One of his suggestions is, *"Take calculated risks. That is quite different from being rash."* Athletes learn to work through hardships and strengthen their resolve. They learn about their strengths and weaknesses when they lose. They have to take calculated risks.

7.7 Play to Win Rather Than Not to Lose

When you try not to lose, you have given up the aggressive mode that is required to win. You are telling your opponent that you are tired. It gives an incentive to your opponent to beat you. One of Eric Hoffer's[37] quotes is, *"You can discover what your enemy fears most by observing the means he uses to frighten you."* In sports, the team that tries to play its opponents game, rather than its own, usually loses. Winners in sports (and in politics) know how take their opponents out of their comfort zones.

7.8 Recruiters and Coaches

The best recruiters may not be the best coaches and vice versa. Winning head coaches have integrity. They are good teachers. They know their game and weaknesses. Even though they may not have been stars in their prime. They can handle their emotional athletes. They learn from their failures. Good coaches cannot win without good athletes and assistants. Recruiting good athletes is one of the primary goals of any coach and is the life blood of university sports. Talent and physical attributes of athletes are innate. Coaches can only teach the mechanics. A good coach pushes his players do their best on and off the court.

7.9 Sports Is a Business, and So Is Life

Sports, in this country, is a big business taking in billions of dollars. If a university has a national champion team, or even a top-ten team, alumni will pour money into that university's coffers. Universities and professional teams in this country attract top athletes from all over the world to play at the college and at the professional levels. An athlete that helps his teammate better makes his team successful. Same is true with married couples. In life, as in sports, winners cut their losses.

7.10 Treatment of Professional Athletes and Career Professionals

Most treat professional athletes differently than career professionals. Professional teams trade their athletes like products. Fans adore successful athletes, which lasts as long as they are successful. Even though fans do not know a successful athlete, they refer to him by his first name. People refer to a professional by his last name with respect.

It is very difficult in dealing with an emotional opponent. One way is simply smile when the opponent makes a mistake. This makes him more irritated causing him to make more mistakes. This works in sports and in any work place.

7.11 Gambling

Gambling is dangerous to you, your family, and to your future. It is addictive. Unfortunately, many of the states in this country have legalized gambling. The ones who get hurt are the poor and the uneducated. They think they can get rich by gambling. Casinos use psychology to lure gamblers to get them started and get hooked on the possibility of riches. The house, i.e., the casino, wins on the average.

Modern gambling is playing the stock market. People have made money by studying the market, looking into indexes that give a measure of price-to-earnings ratios, trends and other aspects. Most are neither capable nor have the time to study the market. Mutual funds invest in several companies pooled together. This allows the principle of averaging. Direct investment in the stock market is good only for professionals.

7.12 Clichés in Sports and in Life

Coaches use clichés to train their players to have a winning attitude and play to their potential. They encourage them to be magnanimous when they win and gracious when they lose. Coach Lombardi[38] used to say, *"The spirit, the will to win, and the will to excel are the things that endure."* Teachers use clichés to raise curiosity and motivation to learn in their students. Preachers use them to encourage their congregations to follow God's teachings. Politicians use them to get the support of their constituents. Leaders in the armed forces use them to build aggressiveness and get the troops ready for a conflict.

It is better to be underestimated than overestimated by your opponent. In sports, if you made a mistake early, you have a chance to correct it later in the match. This applies to life also. On one-on-one competition, in sports, or in politics, the one's that gets into the opponent's head and control his opponent's actions will win. Unfortunately, if this happens in married life, it will have deleterious effects on the family.

7.13 One Part Affects Other Parts of the Sport, Just Like in Life

When two teams are close to each other in talent, the team that has the defense and offense complementing each other invariably wins. When a wife and husband work together in life like two wings of a bird in flight, they will be successful and happy. In sports, as in life, mistakes are often costlier than successes they may bring.

7.14 Secrecy in Professional Life

You do not show your cards to your opponents in a poker game. In professional life, you will be in competition with your associates. Do not be an open book to all your associates. If you are, they know all your moves, while you do not know theirs.

Chapter Eight:
Common Sense Values

Basics:

8.1 Human Ingenuity

Nature gave humans a brain and talents to use to survive and flourish. With human ingenuity, we learn to swim, build vehicles that help us soar in the sky and travel on oceans, and go to the moon. We communicate with others who are far away through space. We can accomplish more and more by using our brains.

8.2 Nature Compensates for Inadequacies

Nature may not provide all the faculties of the human need. A child may be blind or deaf or have some other inadequacy. In that case, nature sharpens other senses. For instance, a blind person may have more abilities in his hearing than a normal person. A mentally challenged one may have a sense of recognizing a nice individual that would not harm him. We cannot control nature, but we can learn to live within the constraints.

8.3 Money

Most would rather have more money than not. It is worth having if used properly. It has no real value if not used wisely. Use it as a tool to help yourself and family in achieving your goals. Help your children only if they know how to use it wisely. It is a source of conflicts in families. It blinds people and is one of the root causes of evils in this world. Some of the conflicts may be caused by one group having more money than another group and indirectly suppressing one over the other group.

One of John D. Rockefeller's[39] quotes is, "*I know nothing more despicable and pathetic than a man who devotes all the hours of the waking day to the making of money for money's sake.*" Help the needy. No one takes money with them when they die.

8.4 Do Not Go Away from Basics and Your Ideals

Basics do not change. Do not go too far from basics. Do not sway away from your ideals. Believe in yourself and recognize your strengths and weaknesses. Do the right thing the first time. Keep your moral compass focused. When you water a tree, you water the roots of the tree and not the leaves. Sometimes in life, one has to go against convention. It is like going into wind, or floating upstream in a river. In life, when there is a problem, attend to the root cause of the problem rather than treat it superficially.

8.5 Everyone Needs Space

We all keep an aura of sanctity around us. Aura is our spiritual signature. If you are having a conversation with someone, you have a sense of how close you can be in proximity with that individual. There is an invisible barrier between the participants. Give proper comfort space to everyone, especially to your family and friends. Don't put your family or your friends in awkward situations. Don't try to enter the solemn space of someone dear to you by asking probing questions that he or she is uncomfortable about.

8.6 Confidence and Prioritization

Without confidence, you are powerless. Build your confidence by doing your homework. Talent is important, but preparation is just as important in anyone's success.

In prioritizing your plans, make sure the plans make a difference for you, your family, and your organization. Order activities according to how much difference they make in your life and others depending on you. Give your maximum effort to important items. Be positive, but not Pollyannaish. There are going to be minor irritations to deal with; prepare for them. Minimize your nervous energies whenever possible. Samuel Johnson[40] states, "*Self-confidence is the first requisite to great undertakings.*"

8.7 Time and Place

Some events in life appear randomly in time and place. In reality, though, you get only a few chances to succeed or fail. You fail at times because either you were not ready or you were not at the right place at the right time. Know your constraints.

I have come across many outstanding young engineers (men) who worked hard during their study and did well in college but did not look for their mates even though in college, there is a large pool of young women to court. After they started working, there was a small pool of women to be acquainted with. Some politicians either wait too long or jump in too early in election contests. Their success rate is low. A winner knows when to get into an election contest. Events generally dictate one's actions. Prepare to achieve your goals and time them properly.

8.8 Beauty is only Skin-deep

Many young men look for the beauty, but one has to think about long-range effects of any activity. An old saying is, *"Beauty is only skin-deep, but it is in the eye of the beholder."* Many of the smart men do not like pretty women, as they can be centers of attraction to other men. Many of the wives of athletes, politicians, attorneys, and public figures tend to be good-looking. Politicians need to have attractive wives to be in public. Athletes attract beautiful women because of their physique. Attorneys and politicians are good on their feet and have attractive spouses.

The wives of the ones who have gone through hard knocks in life may not be as pretty. These worked hard during their college days and did not have time to attract young women. They tend to marry late. When they were ready to settle, the pool was small. An important lesson they learned in life, whether finding a spouse, a real friend, or an employer, in searching for the one that makes them better in every sense is hard. Finding a spouse with common sense is a good first step in life!

8.9 Perception and Reality

In life, some like everyone to believe they are carrying their organization on their shoulders and the organization cannot survive without them. They forget the reality that everyone is replaceable. Everyone in this world is here for a short time!

Watch what a person does and not what he says. Actions speak louder than words.

Perception is stronger than reality until the later kicks in, and then the reality takes over. It is not easy to change the impression of an individual, especially the first one. The good reputation is changed by a single misstep by the individual. It is good to use personal progress as a measure. Comparing with others will make one unhappy.

General Thoughts:
8.10 Happiness

Happiness is a journey, not a destination. It comes from inside. Unhappiness comes when expectations exceed realities. Some do certain things as they feel it is their duty. They may complain, but they get happiness by completing their endeavors. Others find reasons for not doing their jobs. No one can help them unless they help themselves and find their own path to success and happiness. Happy people do things because they want to. Accepting the realities of life is hard. We are forced to sometime.

W. H. Auden[41] states, "*No human being can make another one happy.*"

8.11 Happy and Sad People

Happy people look at things on the brighter side. For them, life seems to be short. Sad people look at the dark side. For them, life seems never ending. The old proverb "*Is the glass half-empty or half-full*" depends upon the perspective and attitude of the individual. Interestingly, engineers may say the glass is twice as big as it needs to be! We must have a balanced view in life. Vulnerability is a part of human nature.

8.12 Height of Insanity

The height of insanity is doing the same thing repeatedly and expecting a new result each time. This is what gamblers expect.

8.13 Sayings of an Old Farmer and a Geologist

A farmer friend who was not-well-to-do used to complain about his mother-in-law, his land, and everything else in this world. His land was not fertile. His crops did not do as well as many others. He used to complain that his mother-in-law favored his sister-in-law. He used to say that mother-in-law and Mother Earth are the most partial in life.

An unsuccessful geologist complained about the Mother Earth in similar terms, as most of the holes he was drilling were dry holes. There is a similarity between the poor farmer friend and the unsuccessful geologist. The farmer and the geologist are poor but not the land. The farmer can make his land a better farmland by fertilizing it, and the geologist can find a better hole to drill for oil by using his noggin.

8.14 Prejudices and Human Instincts

No one knows how long prejudice has been in our way of life. It is a societal based phenomenon. Prejudice can be based on skin color, ethnicity, gender, and other aspects of human life. Prejudiced ones do not know how discrimination hurts unless they have gone through it themselves. Children do not know prejudice, as it is acquired.

Economic factors are a major part of prejudices in people. It is easy to say that whites are prejudiced against blacks. What can you say about the prejudices Catholics and Protestants have in Ireland, the prejudices in India between Hindus and Muslims, the prejudices in Yugoslavia between Serbs and Croats, and the prejudices between Muslims and Jews in the Middle East? Religion seems to be one of the problems. Economics, more than anything else, creates prejudices, and they in turn create conflicts.

8.15 Bigots' Comments on Women

Bigots make derogatory comments about everyone, especially women. A bigot used to say, *"A woman's place is home. The proof is the man has an outdoor toilet and a woman has an indoor toilet. The ratio of the trunk of a man versus his height is smaller compared to the same ratio of a woman. The center of gravity of a man is in his shoulder, whereas for a woman, it is in her hips. Nature provides body space for a woman to bear children. Women's bodies are complicated and are physically weaker than men."* Nature compensates women by providing them with better intelligence than men. They are better judges of human behavior than men. One of Lord Byron's[42] quotes is, *"Those who will not reason, are bigots, those who cannot, are fools, and those who dare not, are slaves."*

8.16 Life Can Be Unfair

Life is not always fair. It gets worse if one of your feet is in the past and one is in the present. Strive for the best from what you have. If you have disabilities, learn to circumvent them. Nature helps the ones who give their best. People will help you, if you are good-natured and are willing to accept their help.

Proud ones do not like any help. Successful ones take help from all. Taking help from others is not a charity.

W. Somerset Maugham[43] states, *"It is a funny thing about life, if you refuse to accept anything but the best, you very often get it: if you utterly decline to make do with what you get, then somehow or other you are very likely to get what you want."*

8.17 Affluence, Power, and Status Corrupt People

Affluence corrupts one's basic values. It causes people to think they are better than the less privileged ones. Rich and powerful countries exerted themselves by invading other countries throughout history. This behavior ruined countries over time.

Power corrupts more than affluence. People with power do things they can get away with. If they do, they not only fail in their life, they also embarrass their family and friends. Status in society gives individuals a platform to succeed only in the short run.

8.18 Luck or Planned Success

Many appear to be in the right place at the right time. Is it luck? Alternatively, is it the result of a well-planned event? It is luck if one wins a lottery, as the odds of this are very small. There are many examples in life that are random. Finding a mate that matches one's interest is like throwing a die. That is like flipping a coin. See the skyrocketing divorce rate in this country, which is approximately 50 percent.

If you plan and work hard with persistence, you will earn what you are looking for. There is no way to quantify the measure of luck. Miracles do happen and they come in the form of coincidences. Roy D. Chapin, Jr.[44] suggests, *"Be ready when opportunity comes…luck is the time when preparation and opportunity meet."* Success comes with privileges. Privilege breeds pressure. Misusing them brings damages to the individual, family, and the associated organization. In life, hard-earned memories last a long time!

8.19 Knowledge, Wealth, and Power

An elderly man, who immigrated from one of the East European countries to this country, told me his past story. He used to be wealthy. The Nazis took all his personal property away. After that, he made a promise to himself to pursue something that nobody would or could ever take away from him. He decided to get education. Wealth and power can be taken away; knowledge can never be taken away. It is like parents' love.

One of John Wesley's well-known quotes, a basis to the Methodist's principles, is, "*Do all the good you can. By all the means you can. In all the ways you can. In all the places you can. To all the people you can. As long as ever you can.*"

8.20 Small Businesses

Small businesses are the engines for the prosperity of any country. They are the lifeblood of a community, a county, a state, and, in general, a country. Starting a small business is a daunting experience. Being an apprentice is the best way to learn a small business before owning one. The owner has to take care of finances to run the business, managing the employees, and, most importantly, dealing with customers. At the end of the day, if things are working the way they should, it is rewarding to the owner that he is helping others, and, at the same time, rewarding himself. Small businesses do well if they treat their employees and customers like their family members. If the employees are properly treated, they will make sure that the business will thrive. Customers in any business activity are always right. Do not over charge or sell your services cheap. Do not underestimate an unhappy customer. If the customer is satisfied, he will recommend your business to others. Initial and final contact with your customer defines the future relationship. Repeat customers are the bread and butter of any business venture.

The owner of a small business should take part in its important activity. For example, the owner of a restaurant should either be a cook or attend the cash register. John David Wright[45] describes business activity as, "*Business is like riding a bicycle. Either you keep moving or you fall down.*" Building a small business requires spending one's life savings and time, sacrificing and giving blood and sweat by the entire family.

8.21 Restaurants

If you want to open up a new restaurant, look for a location convenient for your customers. At the low end, many may not have cars or leisure time. If the restaurant is a quick eatery place, locate it near a high school, college, or industry. If the restaurant is an expensive restaurant, locate it in a nice location. Customers who want to have a nice time do not mind driving a few miles to find a good restaurant. If the location is good and pleasant, customers will pay extra. If you offer the same food like others on the block, then there is no incentive for the customers to look for your restaurant.

In recent years, all you can eat buffet type restaurants have popped up in this country. People tend to eat more than they should at these places, creating obesity in young and old. In addition, it is sad to see the waste at these eateries.

The connection between the customer and the patron are the waiters. Pay them well, keep them interested in your business, and get their advice in improving customer relations. If a new customer comes in, send him a note thanking him for his visit to your restaurant and give a coupon for his next visit.

Customers are the best advertisers in any business!

8.22 Ethnic Restaurants

If you are looking for an ethnic restaurant, find a restaurant that is popular with the people of that ethnicity. For example, if you see many Chinese eating at a Chinese restaurant, it is an indication that it is good.

Chapter Nine:

Life's Simple Lessons

Life:
9.1 Simple Life
We age and die, as we are mortals. Find an opportunity to laugh. In later life, we worry why we did not do more. You cannot change your past, not even a second ago. Do not worry about things that you do not have any control over, or cannot do anything about. Follow the old saying, *"Don't sweat the small stuff."* Do not give up your dreams. When you do, that is the end. A simple life is easier on our nerves and we live longer.

Albert Schweitzer[46], one of the greatest humanitarians, said, *"I ask knowledge what it can tell me of life. Knowledge replies that what it can tell me is little, yet immense. Whence this universe came, whither it is bound, or how it happens to be at all, knowledge cannot tell me. Only this: that the will-to-live is everywhere present even as in me."*

9.2 Conduct and Behavior
Conduct yourself in a way so that your family, friends, and colleagues will be proud to associate with you. Be truthful to yourself, your family, friends, and associates. Be kind to the ones that are not as endowed as you are. If you are honored for your help to the needy, be proud of it, and keep up your good work. One of the Portuguese sayings is, *"Better to deserve honor and not have it than to have honor and not deserve it."*

Bad behavior propagates faster than good behavior. It takes a long time to build a monument and a short time to wreck it. It is easy to slide down a hill, but it takes an effort to go uphill. It is easier to float down the river than it is to paddle up the river. It is easy to follow the wind in a sailboat, whereas it takes effort and ingenuity to sail against the wind. It is easier to fail than to succeed.

9.3 Freedom

Freedom with boundaries is wonderful when used with respect. This includes freedom of press, economic freedom, political freedom, individual freedom, family freedom, etc. Over the centuries, people have lived in many forms of government. A country controlled by citizen-elected officials is the best if governed according to laws. The laws are supposed to protect the freedom of the citizenry, and the laws of the state bind them. An anonymous saying is, "*Freedom is a gift that must be earned.*"

No one wants to live in a country or in a society where there is no liberty to do the things they want to do. Most societies provide boundaries and expect their members to respect the boundaries. Life without boundaries creates chaos. You do not have freedom if you do not have self-control. You are the only one who can find out how to control yourself. No one can teach you that. If you lost self-control in any argument, you lost the argument. Self-mastery helps you succeed. Economic freedom helps to achieve other freedoms. Everyone wants to be free and not to be a subservient to anyone!

Old Age:
9.4 Getting Old

As we get older, our reaction time gets longer. We developed common sense throughout our lives and give it to our children and to anyone who wants to listen. We make mistakes and remember less. We forget where we left our eyeglasses, keys, and yes, important papers, the previous night. If we put them in a specific place before bed time every day and making it a habit helps us. We question why we do the things that do not have immediate results. We need to be at ease and lenient with others making mistakes. We get satisfaction by helping others. Look at every day as a Sunday.

We are interested in the history of the family and wish the best for the family. We become more spiritual, not necessarily religious, and want to help others. As our memory issues become serious, we need to accept the realities, even though it is painful to us and to the family. Becoming defensive is counterproductive. We hate it when someone tells us that we can do something we did in the past and cannot do it now. We like to do things that come easy and avoid conflicts if at all possible. Kindness to an old person by anyone, especially by a young one, makes that individual's spirits high.

Our life story is an open book to anyone. Family's future depends upon how smooth the transition from one generation to the next. Delegating to younger generation provides self-satisfaction for us. It is a step in making a smooth transition. We feel better if they get the perception that our advice is important to the family. We know, in the final analysis, the family members will and can to take care of themselves.

9.5 Growing Old Is Not For Sissies

When one is old, he is like an old car. Fix one part of the body and another part go bad. In a marathon race of life, last third is a lot harder than the first two-thirds of life. The end does not happen until the person gives up. It is like riding a bike. If you do not keep peddling, you lose balance and fall. Trying to adapt to new situations and environments is difficult for seniors. Elders need to keep their mind active and body fit to their best of ability. Quality of life becomes more important than simply living. The best exercises are, if possible, walking and thinking about life while walking.

9.6 Modern Countries and Their Elderly

Modern countries are taking strides to take care of their elderly. Unfortunately, the laws cannot change the day-to-day life of old people. They like to live quietly. Their physical constraints do not allow them to be free and have time to advise anyone. They know what is right and what could go wrong. They were successful in their earlier part of their life and think about the past. They are helpless and feel trapped in their bodies. Medical science has been diligent in helping humans live longer. It comes to a point that quality of living is more important than just living. They ask what life is all about and no one can answer. Their comfort range narrows; memory issues become prominent; like to leave this world with dignity; and hope the end comes sooner than later. Taking care of the elderly is difficult, as they often do not feel well. They become child-like and become cantankerous. Laughter is the best medicine. Little children can provide that.

9.7 Loneliness

Loneliness is the ultimate poverty no one can endure. The older generation takes the brunt. In the Western world, the economy is good and younger ones move away. Senior citizens want to have their family nearby. Life with no laughter or children is an empty life. Mother Teresa[47] sates, "*The most terrible poverty is loneliness and the feeling of being unloved.*" In third world countries, agriculture is the major occupation for living. Younger generations stay close to their families and the elderly is happy. In the modern world, people tend to care about their pets than with their own older family members.

9.8 Support Groups

Most support would come from one's family members. If they are far away, building a support group from neighbors, friends, and colleagues is necessary. They can give support, sometimes moral support, during the time of adversity. Without a support group, one is alone like the one in an open field during a lightning storm. Fortunately, there are social support groups that are eager to help and can direct anyone to find help.

9.9 Clinics and Hospitals

When you are sick, these places are wonderful. If you are not sick and you are accompanying a sick person, two thoughts may come to mind. You feel sorry for the sick people, and you feel good that you are healthy. Maintenance of your body is the key in reducing illnesses just as it is for your car or your house or your family. It is good to have a primary doctor whose judgment you respect. If you do not have good health, you have no life and you are of no help to anyone.

There is less attention given to mental frailties compared to physical frailties by the society in general, as the physical frailties are outwardly visible.

Common Sense:
9.10 Leverage

Gadgets have been invented throughout human history to survive, prosper, and make a good living. Education is the first step in achieving one's goals. Technology had an exponential growth, improving human life, in the past fifty years and has not slowed down. Technology moves much faster than the social movements.

Psychological leverage is a part of human nature as well. Teachers say that if you do not study, you will not pass the course. Elected politicians will provide funding if they are voted in. Voters will vote a politician out of office if he does not follow their wishes. Contractors say that if you do not pay the bill, they put a lien on your house. The owners say we are not going to pay you if you do not do what you are supposed to do. There is no black-and-white situation in most cases. If you have the right reasons and are not getting the proper response from a contractor, contact the government official in your community. If you can get him to see your problem, you will generally get the problem resolved. The contractor is concerned about his license to do the work in the community. If you do not have a strong case, it is better to compromise.

9.11 Losing Battle

Fight only for right causes. If you are in a fight, do your best to win. Choosing the battle you can win is tricky. Pres. Thomas Jefferson[48] stated, "*In matter of style, I will swim with the tide and be happy to compromise, but in matters of principle, I will stand like a rock.*" Mahatma Gandhi[49] described himself, as "*I am not a visionary. I claim to be a practical idealist.*"

9.12 Small or Large Portions

It is better to do exercises in shorter intervals periodically than doing them at longer intervals irregularly. You learn more by periodically studying than cramming. Doctors prescribe medicine that is to be taken periodically, as large doses can kill anyone. Everyone eats food one spoon at a time and not the whole meal in one swallow.

9.13 Thinking in the Old and in the Modern World

An Oriental student was appalled about a university president's interest in taking his old position as a professor. In third-world countries, leaders have to go up or retire. Fame lasts longer in third-world countries compared to the West. On fame, Jacob Burckhardt's[50] says, "*Fame, which flees the man who seeks it, overtakes the man who is heedless of it.*" Pres. George Washington, an eminent leader, retired to his farm after his presidency. He even could have made himself a king. Instead, he chose a simple life.

9.14 Eccentric Ones

Everyone has different ideas in describing eccentric people. Financial freedom allows for individualism and eccentricities. A rich man is eccentric if his behavior pattern does not fit the norm of society, whereas a poor man with the same behavior pattern is crazy. A highly educated person, such as a professor at a university, with unusual behavior patterns is a genius, whereas an uneducated person with the same behavioral pattern is an idiot. Dealing with or living with an eccentric individual is very difficult.

An extreme case of eccentricity is mental illness. Living with people with mental illness is like living in hell. Family and friends are sympathetic if a person is physically sick, whereas they tend to be intolerant if he is mentally ill. Mentally ill ones can hurt or even kill others and themselves. Physically ill ones cannot hurt others. Society needs to focus more on the people's mental health, as it is hard to diagnose early and treat.

Developed countries tolerate eccentric behavior more than poor countries. Eccentric people have crazy ideas, as they do not fit the normal pattern of the day even though they may be right. Research (Re-search) by its meaning is searching old ideas to find new ways. Geniuses look at things in a way that no one did before. They tend to be eccentric, and have ideas that revolutionize some current thinking. Many of these are inventors. Thomas Alva Edison[51], a patron saint of inventors said, *"Genius is one percent inspiration and ninety-nine percent perspiration. Accordingly, a 'genius' is often merely a talented person who has done all of his or her homework."*

9.15 Chadastam

"Chadastam" is a Telugu word used to describe a behavior pattern of a person how things should be done. People with this syndrome want to have things done in a certain way, i.e., their way and no other way. They tend to be very smart and dominate others who are weak. They are honest, smart, and hard-driving. They are perfectionists. They are real *"characters."* Chadastam is a trait, an inherited characteristic, from one generation to the next. They can be categorized as somewhere between eccentric and crazy, sometimes referred to as ones with *a screw loose*. They make the lives of people miserable. One way they do this is by biting the *"head off"* of their prey if they do or say something they do not like. They repeat their wishes to be known over-and-over to no end. All of us have our own idiosyncrasies (or some refer to them as *"idiot-syn-*

crasies"). Some cannot help themselves to get over their worst fears and habits. Understand and deal with people with this in mind. Build bridges, not walls, in dealing with people.

9.16 Men and Women

In the past, it was normal for women to stay home giving them time to think and analyze on a long-term basis. It is like cooking a meal using a crock-pot. Men had to do things on a short-time basis, as they had to react quickly in the wild. It is like cooking a meal using a microwave oven. Women can analyze men better than men can analyze women. Women are forced to multiplex their activities, i.e., do things in parallel with children and family activities, whereas men tend to do their activities one after another.

When the married couple is young, the young lady follows the man admiring his intellect and his strength and the man adores his wife for her beauty and thoughtfulness. In most cases, husbands are older than wives. When the couple becomes old, the man follows the lady. In the later years of couple's life, the husband's strength and memory weakens and depends on his wife. An old saying is, "*If the husband died first, the wife lives long after his death. If the wife died first, the husband's death comes quickly.*"

9.17 Structure and Change

Nature is unique, authentic with a structure. The sun comes up in the east and goes down in the west. We come into existence, have life, and die. Humans have invented mathematics and science. Without them, we will be living in the Stone Age. Society has structure with a government with laws, taxing structure, et cetera. Without structure, we have chaos. Each human being is unique. Successful ones make use of the structure and the constant change to grow and make their life better one day to the next.

Without change, life will be boring. Nature provides constant change. It has its own destructive side. There are tornadoes, floods, earthquakes, volcanoes, fires, etc. Nature is selective in its path of destruction. No one should underestimate nature's fury.

Unfortunately, there are some humans that are detriment to others. To control the undesired ones, society has police forces. In a similar manner, countries have armed forces to safeguard their citizens from undesired forces from other countries. These forces are trained to face head-on to the dangers, and even knowingly risk their lives in safe guarding their fellow citizens. Normal human nature is run away from danger. Policemen, firemen, and soldiers should have our highest respect for their work.

Most difficult times in one's life are the uncertainties during transitions of any kind. This may be during different stages of life, wherein one wishes a better life or even afraid of what could or would happen. A change in one's job or losing one's loved one, or anyone of myriad things one could imagine, could affect one's life. Everyone in transition should consider the possibility of failures and not lured by the mirage of successes. Our DNA makes us what we are. In the final analysis, making our life better, and helping the people around us to have a better life, determines the quality of our life.

One of the memorable quotes of Jackie Robinson[52], a hall-of-fame major league baseball player, is, *"A life is not important except in the impact it has on another life."*

Chapter Ten:
General Thoughts

Day-To-Day Life:
10.1 News Media and the Politicians

Most get their news from television instead of newspapers and radio. TV has time constraints on their news. Media has a short memory. They can either enhance or destroy a political candidate. Elections are long job interviews of the electorate. A good politician is a historian, a *word merchant*, a debater, and connects to the hearts of the electorate. He does not promise any that he cannot deliver. He tries not to be pinned down to any statement. Pinning down a politician is like trying to pick mercury from the floor. Never trust politicians who love to hear their own voices like *"Echo"* in Greek mythology.

Some politicians improve their standing by smearing their opposition using *dirty tricks* and the opposition has the burden to disprove them. Negative comments carry in the short term. However, positive comments carry in the long term. Some politicians use *kamikaze* type attacks to destroy their opponents. They generally lose. Organization, planning, and good ideas are necessary in winning elections. External events may decide the outcomes in elections. Better to have a statesman as a leader than a politician!

10.2 Plan Your Time in America

You want to go to a discount store to shop. If you go at the peak time, you will be shopping with long line of shoppers bumping into each other. Go when the stores are not busy. If you are going to work driving just before 8:00 A.M.

or just after 5.00 P.M., you will be in a traffic jam. Many companies use flextime, wherein you come and go at the best time. If you do not have flextime at your company, go to work early and leave late. The total time out of your home will be the same either way. You will get more of your work done when other people are going through traffic and enjoy peace at the office. Use car pools or public transportation whenever possible.

Going to restaurants at certain times is another problem. Going early or late gives you better service. In case of motels, it is better to make reservations early and have peace of mind for an overnight stay. Most of the cheaper rooms in a motel are taken first by early reservations. In addition, you may not be able to find a motel room at a late hour.

Do not arrange your meetings the day after a holiday. Arrange two days after a holiday. It provides flexibility to arrange or even cancel for unusual circumstances. It is best to have a doctor's appointment at the earliest time in the morning. The doctor will be more attentive to your needs. In addition, waiting time is minimal.

If you want to spread fertilizer on your lawn, look for rain and avoid watering the lawn. Plan and make your life simple by using simple common sense based ideas!

10.3 Visiting Friends and Relatives

Visiting someone else's home puts burden on the hosts. Before coming for an overnight visit or longer, the visitor should make sure that the lady of the house is ok for such a visit. If not, it would make the visit uncomfortable for the visitor and the hosts. Longer one stays, the less welcome he or she will be. Staying one afternoon and a night gives enough time for a visit. If you are a family member or a best friend, staying two nights works well. Women like staying longer at other people's homes, whereas men like to stay the least amount of time at other's homes. This may be because men survived in the wild while women stayed home in the early stages of mankind.

Children and their families can stay longer at their parents' house. Parents staying at their children's houses should be shorter. The relationship between parents and children is not a bilateral relationship. Parents have a total commitment to their children, whereas the children have comparatively less interest in their parents, as they have commitments to their own children. Staying at the parents' house brings back many good memories. The in-laws have a different take. The shorter their stay is, the better it is for all involved. Parents are guests at their children's homes.

Benjamin Franklin puts it, *"Guests, like fish, begin to smell after three days."*

10.4 Court Cases

In this country, filing a court case does not imply that you are going to win even if you are right. The benefactors in any court proceedings are the attorneys. Even if you win your case, it is expensive in terms of money and mental strain on you and your family. It does not mean that you should lie down and let the other party walk over you. Consider all the costs and then proceed. If you are willing to pay that price, go for it.

10.5 Living in the Midwest and on the East and West Coasts

In this country, economical down turns and up turns start along the coasts. Look for signs of layoffs, hot and cold housing markets, and other trends on the coasts. Midwesterners should take advantage of these early warning signs.

Visualization:
10.6 Still Camera Freezes Life

It is important that we keep a record of our lives, children's lives, relatives' lives, and friends' lives. You can never go back in life, even a second. You can enjoy what was in the past through pictures. Film freezes life. Do not try to rewrite the past. Accept what it was; do not deny the facts of the past; and make the best out of it. An old saying is, *"The past is a prison for those who live in it."*

10.7 Machines and Humans

Computers are here to use for almost every possible situation. These days, students would rather use a computer program to solve a problem than use pencil and paper. If students understand the solution and use the computer as a tool, then it is ideal. Some feel that it is waste of time to learn how to do a problem if you can learn using a computer to achieve the same goal. If we follow this procedure, our understanding becomes service-oriented rather than knowledge-oriented. We might as well replace humans with machines. We may survive for a while but will lose at the end.

For ease and cost, security agencies use computers more and more and humans less and less. Computers cannot replace humans although they can help humans to solve routine problems. Security agencies require the human touch to change quickly when it is necessary. Data in computers requires constant human interface to stay up-to-date.

10.8 Words and Images

We look at an individual and recognize him but cannot remember his name. We use different techniques, such as visualizing his name, thinking aloud his first name, etc.

Using images to replace words helps to achieve goals. Olympic athletes win their races by using mental images of winning before they even start the races. A basketball player has the image of the ball going into the hoop before the ball leaves his hands putting him in a zone. The ones who made a lot of money have the mental image of holding money in their hands. Successful ones have a burning desire, create a picture in their mind, and set deadlines to achieve their goals. Repeating it aloud forces one to find a way to achieve one's goal. What we heard with our ears stays with us; what we saw with our eyes, we can never un-see it; and what we wrote is permanent.

10.9 Children from Ghettos

When you see children from the ghettos, you can look at their eyes and see that their eyes are dull. The same is true about children in some of the third world countries. They do not have any hope. You can only feel sorry for them.

Behaviors:
10.10 Human Responses

Life is what you make out of it with what you have. We hear good and bad news. It is hard to forget bad news or bad treatment. Successful ones have developed their mind to forget bad situations as fast as possible. Unsuccessful ones cannot forget anything bad and tend to mull it repeatedly making it worse and worse. To become happy and productive, learn to develop your mind so that it dampens bad news and enhances the pleasures of good news. Remember that sometimes external events control our life.

10.11 Older Folks from the Third World and the Western World

The older generations from third world countries show their affection to their nearest kin overtly compared to the ones in the Western World. The old ones, especially the men, tend to be stubborn in both worlds.

The ones in the last stages of life everywhere have strong convictions. If they feel that it does not make any difference what they think, their life will end soon.

10.12 Human Conflicts

Humans create conflicts. There are always two sides to every story. To have a child you need a male and a female. To have electricity, you need an electric socket and a plug. To sew, you need a needle and a thread. Humans can resolve conflicts, if they so desire. This requires compromise, patience, and understanding.

Before coming to a conclusion, make sure you know the full story of the conflict. Try to understand someone's behavior by investigating why an individual behaves the way he does. Put yourself in his shoes before you criticize him.

Two of the human passions are love and hatred. We are born out of love. We learn to hate during our growing years due to fear, envy, revenge, prejudice, racism, religious intolerance, etc. Unfortunately, these fears bring out the worst in humans resulting in conflicts and wars that are inevitable. Hate can only be conquered by love!

10.13 Memories in This World

The leaders in the commercial world always ask the question, *"What have you done for us lately?"* The past does not seem to be important. They want you to show constant progress, which is an unattainable goal. This attitude may improve the short-term economy at an expense, but it also creates false hopes.

In third world countries, memory is long. People there hang on to old values. They respect the elders and old traditions. They have many religious festivals, allowing the families to get together. They prefer family over economics. The younger generation in the third world sees the modern world through movies and gadgets. They are eager to jump into the modern ways of the future. They like to make money, but they are in a quandary, somewhere between the old and the new. They forget the good values in their own society. If they can pick the best from both worlds, they will benefit. They know the problems in the third world and see the progress in the West.

In this country we have occasions to get together too during Thanksgiving times and religious holidays. Some of the family members may be living in faraway places, making it difficult to get together. Citizenry enjoys getting together for any occasion.

10.14 Young and Old in This Country

The United States of America is the greatest country in the world. With all the freedom in this country, I would not want to live anywhere else. We have all the comforts in the world. Even the ones that do not have a steady job probably can survive from food stamps, unlike their counterparts in the third world countries.

The future depends on our children. They should have the best education possible. Many high school students have too much free time. They do not know what they want to do with themselves in their free time. This results in boredom and, as a result, they get into a wrong crowd. With many of the parents working, the teenagers have no one to consult except the wrong crowd! As a result, they experiment with drugs, sex, and other illegal activities. I believe the more structure the teenagers have, the better they will be. Schools should provide and encourage extra-curricular activities and parents should take an active part in their children's activities. The more we do at the early stages of our children's lives, the more productive our children will be with their lives.

Older generation brought us into the world and raised us. They look forward to letters from their children and grandchildren. They are our immediate past and we are indebted to them. The best present we can give them is spend quality time with them.

10.15 Everyone Wins Sometimes and Loses at Other Times

Opportunities do not come all the time. For example, elections come every two or four years. If you lose an election, you have to wait until the next time. Running for offices is not for the weak. Watch for the stress and the strain on your family. Success comes to the tenacious and to the goal oriented. When things go bad, wait, and they do turn around. Do not lose hope. Do not give up. Your time will come.

Nature:
10.16 Life Cycle

Perspectives change with age. Life goes in several stages:

A helpless child.

A teenager thinks that he (or she) knows more than anyone else.

A young adult begins to understand life.

An adult who knows the burdens of being a parent and enjoys children.

A grandfather (or grandmother) passes the torch to his (or her) next generation and looks forward to the successes of his (or her) children and grandchildren.

During later stages of life, attachments to the family of birth intensify and deepen. He (or she) is helpless and wishes to leave this world like a ripened fruit fall from a tree and not a burden on the family. Hopes the end comes sooner than later!

Life ends when one gives up and joins his/her ancestors in the celestial skies.

10.17 Nature Provides Habitats and Humans Change Them

Animals are selective grazers and have a different diet to survive. In the interest of expansion, humans encroach into the animal world. Human population has increased to such an extent that there is very little space for the animals in the wild. Zoos provide habitat for animals. They are confined. Humans developed chemicals that are harmful to animals. Humans should respect animal habitats.

10.18 Time and Space Allow Healing

Time heals physical and mental wounds. Space allows one to understand the situation. No one remembers us by our words, but only by our kind deeds. Conflicts fade allowing for peace. Cooperation is better than confrontation in anyone's actions.

10.19 Time Measures with Young and Old

When you are young, days seem too short. You want to do many things. You want to spend time with your friends in the evening and want to sleep late. The years seem to be too long. You want to grow up fast and be a man. You want everyone to put you on a pedestal. You have very little patience for the inefficient. For you, anyone over twenty seems to be too old to be even working. You have very little time to spend with your parents and grandparents, as you have many obligations and not money to enjoy.

When you are old, your thinking is just the opposite of when you were young. The years seem too short, whereas the days seem to be too long. You want to rest a lot. You tend to think, "*Where have the years gone? What have I done that is worthwhile?*" You can see the end of your future. What are the things you want to do that give you peace in the years you have left? You have time and want to spend it with your children and grandchildren, but they seem to have very little time for you. You have money but do not have the energy to travel or enjoy. You feel like an old machine that needs oil to move smoothly and have a hard time getting up if you sit on the floor.

10.20 When Things Go Wrong, They Go Wrong

When things go well, they seem to continue. When things go bad, they seem to continue. Using sports analogy, we make errors that are forced or unforced or have no control over. Minimize the unforced ones. When a door closes, another door or a window opens. Everything goes in cycles. When things are unbearable, follow the Benedictine Prayer from the fifth century by *Lectio Divina*, comprised of a ladder with four steps...

Reading you should seek;

Meditating, you will find;

Praying, you shall call; and

Contemplating, the door will be opened to you!

10.21 Extremist Groups

In every society, there are extremist groups. Leaders of such groups have extreme views and want everyone to follow them. They are charismatic and can brainwash their followers. They think they know what is right for others and want others to do their dirty work. Unfortunately, their followers cannot think for themselves. They have nothing to lose by joining the extremist groups. They will do whatever the leaders tell them to do. That may include doing atrocities and even killing the innocent. They should understand Henry David Thoreau's[53] quote, and is, *"The evil that men do lives after them."*

10.22 Nature of Cats, Dogs, and Humans

Cats tend to be highly independent. When they get sick in their old age, they die fast. Dogs tend to love and depend on humans. When dogs get old and sick, humans take care of them. Dogs tend to live longer than cats, as they trust their masters. They know when their masters are not in their best moods. In those cases, they lie down next to them and wait for their masters to feel better. When they do, they sense and show their affection. Humans do not let their family members alone when they are in a bad mood. They try to find why they are unhappy, which creates additional problems. Animals kill other animals only for food. Sub humans kill other humans in revenge.

10.23 Nature Gives Warnings

If there is smoke, there is fire nearby. If there are clouds in the sky, there is a possibility for rain. There are symptoms before sickness. If there is a beginning, it will have an end. Nature gives us warnings to prepare for natural disasters. At dire times, Nature provides a leader to help. Man made disasters, such as nuclear disasters, are much harder to predict. They are much more destructive compared to natural disasters.

Nature is selective. It can be cruel. Some has the misfortune of having cancer, or Alzheimer's, or other diseases through no fault of their own. Diseases are destructive on the humans. Today, doctors and scientists are working on new drugs and treatments. If we can, being active and keeping good thoughts would be helpful on our body and on our psyche. One of Henry David Thoreau's[54] quotes is, *"Nature is slow but sure; she works no faster than need be; she is the tortoise that wins the race by her perseverance."*

10.24 Unexplainable Items

Children are mistreated for no reason at all. Some children are born to the rich and powerful and others are born to the poor and feeble. There are many poor children in Africa, Asia, South America, and other continents on the streets begging for food. Others are in orphanages and want to be adopted by loving families. The adopted children leave their siblings behind who may be living in poverty. Why is there such an inequity among the children from the same family? Why is it so hard for some people struggle to achieve and others have an easier time to achieve? Based on thousands of years of experience, Hindu philosophy says that one's karma (fate) dictates what happens to him. No one can prove or disprove it. Everyone comes into this world without his or her knowledge and leaves when their time comes. Not everyone is born equal or treated equally. On the other hand, every dead person is equal to every other dead person!

The Bhagavad Gita is a Hindu scripture. Mahatma Gandhi referred to it as his *"Spiritual Dictionary."* On the back book cover is a verse from the Bhagavad Gita.

Notes on the Quotes[55]

1. WILLIAM PENN (1644-1718). *Some Fruits of Solitude, 234, 1693*

2. ALBERT EINSTEIN (1879-1955). Interview with the author. In George Sylvester Viereck, "What Life Means to Einstein, *Glimpses of the Great,* 1930

3. MILDRED SEYDELL, *Methodist Church Bulletin*, Mt. Pleasant, Michigan

4. REINHOLD NIEBUHR (1892-1971). *"The Serenity Prayer," 1934.*

5. ELIZABETH G. HAINSTOCK, *Teaching Montessori in the Home, 1, 1968*

6. S. TRUETT CATHY, (1921-2014). See for a down to earth quotes and suggestions for businesses in a book titled Eat *Mor Chickin: Inspire More People/It is better to Build Boys Than mend Men/How did you do it, Truett*

7. SIGMOND FREUD (1956-1939). 23 JANUARY 1930. In Smiley Blanton, *Dairy of My Analysis with Sigmund Freud, 1971*

8. ROBERT FROST (1874-1963), Quote attributed

9. BERTRAND RUSSELL (1872-1970). On Education: Especially in Early Childhood, 2, 1926

10. RABINDRANATH TAGORE (1861-1941), Quote attributed

11. VAUVENARGUES (1715-1745). *Reflections and Maxims, 127, 1746, tr. F. G. Stevens, 1940*

12. CALVIN COOLIDGE (1872-1933), Quote attributed

13. HERMANN HESSE (1877-1962). *Demian: The Story of Emil Sinclair's Youth*, 6, 1919, tr. Michael Roloff and Michael Lebeck, 1965

14. GEORGE BERNARD SHAW (1856-1950). *"The Womanly Woman," The Quintessence of Ibsenism, 1891*

15. NAPOLEON HILL (1883-1970), For advice in making money, See his book, "Think and Grow Rich," P. 33, Fawcett Publications, Inc., Greenwich, Conn.

16. BENJAMIN FRANKLIN (1706-1790). *Poor Richards Almanack, October 1745*

17. Winston Churchill (1874-1965), Quote attributed

18. BENJAMIN FRANKLIN (1706-1790), *The Autobiography of Benjamin Franklin*, Washington Square Press, *Inc.* New York, 1964

19. JOHN WOODEN (1910-2010), Quote attributed

20. JAMES RUSSELL LOWELL (1819-1891). "Pope," *My Study Windows*, 1871

21. DALE CARNEGIE (1888-1955), *How to Win Friends and Influence People*, rev. ed. 1.1, 1981 (1936)

22. JOHN F. KENNEDY (1917-1963), Quote attributed

23. Voltaire (1715-1747). "Toleration"(1), *Philosophical Dictionary*, 1764, tr. Theodore Besterman, 1971

24. ARNOLD. J. TOYNBEE (1889-1975). *"A Study of history"*, *12.62, 1961*

25. LORD BYRON (1788-1824), Quote attributed

26. ELBERT HUBBARD (1856-1915). *The Note book of Elbert Hubbard, Opposite p. 113, comp.* Elbert Hubbard II, 1927

27. ARISTOTLE (384-322 B. C.). *Nicomachean Ethics, 9.4*, tr. J.A.K. Thomson, 1953

28. LYNDON B. JOHNSON (1908-1973), Quote attributed to Pres. and Mrs. Johnson

29. SIR JAMES DEWAR (1842-1923), Quote attributed

30. WAYNE GRETZKY (1961-), Quote attributed

31. WARREN BUFFETT (1930-). About Investing: Know the Difference Between Price and Value," *Warren Buffett Speaks: Wit and Wisdom from the World's Greatest Investor*, Comp. Janet Lowe, 1997

32. A. C. GRALING (1949-), "Philosophy with warts," *New York Times Book Review*, 29 December 1996

33. MARTIN LUTHER KING, JR., (1929-1968). Where do we go from here: Chaos or Community? 2.4, 1967

34. JOHN HURTON COLLINS (1848-1908), Quote attributed

35. LEONARDO da VINCI (1452-1519), Quote attributed

36. GEORGE S. PATTON Jr. (1885-1945), Quote attributed

37. ERIC HOFFER (1902-1983), *The Passionate State of Mind: And Other Aphorisms*, 222, 1954

38. VINCE LOMBARDI (1930-1970), Football Coach, Quote attributed

39. JOHN D ROCKEFELLER (1839-1937). In Lewis H. Lapham, *Money and Class in America: Notes and Observations on the Civil Religion*, 8, 1988

40. SAMUEL JOHNSON (1709-1784). "Pope", *Lives of the English Poets*, 1781

41. W. H. AUDEN (1907-1973). "Postscript: The Frivolous & the Earnest," *The Dyer's Hand AND Other Essays*, 1962

42. LORD BYRON (1788-1824), (Was one of the greatest English poets and a leading figure in the Romantic movement), Quote attributed

43. W. SOMERSET MAUGHAM (1874-1965), Quote attributed

44. ROY D. CHAPIN, Jr. (1915-2001), Former Chairman and CEO of American Motors Corporation, Quote attributed

45. JOHN DAVID WRIGHT (1909-1979). President of the Thompson Products, Inc. In Gilbert Burck, "The Rush to Diversity," *Fortune*, September 1955

46. ALBERT SCHWEITZER (1875-1965), Quote attributed

47. MOTHER TERESA (1910-1997), Also, known as Saint Teresa of Calcutta, Quote attributed

48. THOMAS JEFFERSON (1743-1826), Usually quoted attributed to him in the context of home making or education

49. MAHATMA GANDHI (1869-1948). His real name is Mohandas K. Gandhi. Mahatma – A person regarded with reverence or loving respect, a holy person or sage. Quote attributed to him, March 6, 2015

50. JACOB BURCKHARDT (1818-1897). "The Great Men of History," 1870, *Force an and Freedom: An Interpretation, ed.* James A. Nichols, 1943

51. THOMAS ALVA EDISON (1847-1931). *Remark to the* author. In M. K. Rosanoff, Edison in his Laboratory" *Harpers'*, September 1932

52. JACKIE ROBINSON (1919-1972), Quote attributed

53. HENRY DAVID THOREAU (1817-1862), Quote attributed

54. HENRY DAVID THOREAU (1817-1862), Journal, 14 January 1861

55. LEONARD ROY FRANK (1932-2015), For many of the citations I have used the book *"Quotationary"*, Random House, New York, 2001. This book has a collection of over 20,000 quotes and their references. In many cases, the citations of some of the quotes used in this book were not available. I have also used the Internet to find additional information on the quotes. If I could not find the citation of a quote and is well known, I indicated that the quote is attributed.

CPSIA information can be obtained
at www.ICGtesting.com
Printed in the USA
BVHW01s0612190318
510949BV00020BA/303/P